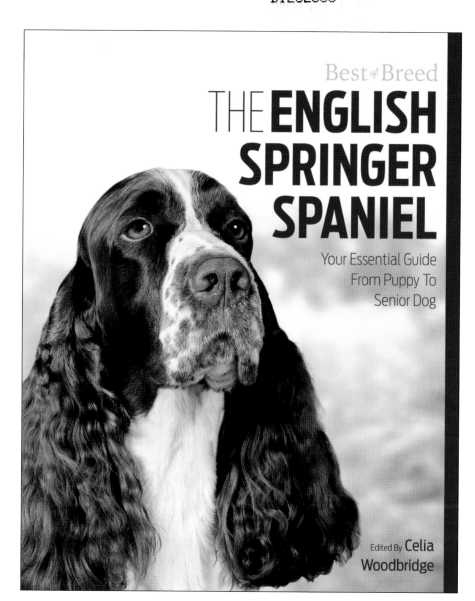

Best of Breed

THE **ENGLISH SPRINGER SPANIEL**

Your Essential Guide
From Puppy To
Senior Dog

Edited By Celia
Woodbridge

ACKNOWLEDGEMENTS
The publishers would like to acknowledge the following for help with photography: Jenny Miller (Feorlig), Gareth Lawler (Roqfolly), Ann Corbett (Trinmere), Jenny Williams (Cobhay), Celia Woodbridge (Crackerjanne), Colin Muirhead (Shipden), English Springer Spaniel Welfare, Hearing Dogs for Deaf People, and Support Dogs.
Thanks also to David Tomlinson for his excellent photos of working English Springer Spaniels.
Page 18 © Metropolitan Police; page 20 © istockphoto.com/Lawrence Sawyer
page 59 © istockphoto.com/Galina Barskaya; Page 92 © istockphoto.com/Galina Barskaya

Cover photo: © Tracy Morgan Animal Photography (www.animalphotographer.co.uk)

The British Breed Standard reproduced in Chapter 7 is the copyright of the Kennel Club and published with the club's kind permission. Extracts from the American Breed Standard are reproduced by kind permission of the American Kennel Club.

THE QUESTION OF GENDER
**The 'he' pronoun is used throughout this book in favour of the rather impersonal 'it',
but no gender bias is intended.**

First published in 2008 by the Pet Book Publishing Company Limited
St Martin's Farm, Chapel Lane, Zeals, Wiltshire BA12 6NZ

Reprinted in 2010 and 2011

This edition first published in 2015

© 2015 Pet Book Publishing Company Limited.
Printed and bound in South Korea.

ISBN
978-1-910488-07-2
1-910488-07-0

CONTENTS

GETTING TO KNOW ENGLISH SPRINGER SPANIELS

Chapter 1

I f you are looking for a companion for walking, working or just generally enjoying life, who will willingly join in most activities with wholehearted enthusiasm, whose eyes mirror his complete devotion, and whose tail wags furiously to show his joy at being alive – particularly in your company – then surely there cannot be a breed more suited to this role than the English Springer Spaniel.

A TYPICAL SPRINGER

An English Springer Spaniel is a medium-sized, lean but powerfully built dog, bred originally for flushing or springing game for the net, falcon or Greyhound. An English Springer should stand at up to 51 cm (20 in) at the shoulder and, at that size, would weigh a maximum of 22.5 kg (50 lb).

The breed's most arresting feature is its head, with a fairly broad top divided by a groove and moderate

The English Springer is a medium-sized sporting dog with a racy build.

stop into a good length of nose, and a strong, square jaw to facilitate the retrieving of heavy game. The Springer has moderately long ears, and a soft, trusting yet intelligent expression in his eyes. He has a weather-resisting coat that is easy to manage and is furnished with moderate feathering on the ears, legs, underbelly and tail. The Springer can be liver and white, black and white, or either of these colours with tan markings. He can be seen with either a full tail, a tail docked to about half its length (a working dock), or shorter still to about a third of its original length.

In the USA the docking of show dogs is customary, but legislation has been passed in the UK that allows only working dogs to have their tails docked. The reason for this exception is that a Springer working in brambles, gorse and thick undergrowth could seriously damage his tail. Not only can the skin be torn, causing the tail to bleed, but also if the tail is too long, the vertebrae in the tail can be fractured. I have owned two dogs who have suffered in this way over the years with the result that their tails had to be docked even further, requiring a serious operation in an adult dog. Dogs docked after April 2007 are not eligible to be shown at any event in the UK where the public pay for admission.

My own opinion of this legislation is that it is misguided. Over the past 40-odd years I have owned many Springer Spaniels, and, like many hundreds of other owners, I have always had the health and welfare of my Springers at heart. I would take a lot of convincing that the people who legislate on such matters, or their advisors, are as knowledgeable as the majority of competent owners.

ESSENTIALLY A WORKING DOG

The Springer Spaniel is a natural hunter and the majority of present-day Springers, if allowed to develop along these lines, are more than willing and able to demonstrate that they have not lost this ability. Retrieving is a natural progression for any hunting dog or animal, in the same way that watching a vixen

We are now getting used to seeing English Springers with full tails.

carrying a rabbit or pheasant back to her cubs is to see a natural retriever. This is quite an experience to view unless you happen to be a gamekeeper, shooting owner or shooting tenant. This aspect of our Springers has been developed over the years so that he can be trained to flush game from cover, not catch it in there, and retrieve it tenderly on command. The tender mouth has been achieved and continued by selective breeding, using only stock that demonstrates this attribute.

Over the years the English Springer Spaniel has developed into two distinct types and it could now be said that the split is complete.

THE SHOW TYPE

The type of Springer Spaniel that competes in the show ring has developed as breeders have tried to produce stock to conform to the Breed Standard, which is the written blueprint for the breed, describing the 'perfect' English Springer. The show type has longer ears, is taller, moves with a steadier gait, and has a 'squarer' look to the muzzle and at the back end than its working counterpart. Any Champions found in the pedigree will be either Sh. Ch. (Show Champion) or Ch. (Champion).

To be recognised as a Show Champion a dog must, in layman terms, win three Challenge Certificates at Championship shows under three separate judges. If the owner then wishes to claim the title Ch. (Champion), his dog must obtain a Gundog Working Certificate. To do this he must demonstrate that he has the basic requirements to be a gundog. For a spaniel he must show that he is not gun shy, that he hunts, faces cover, produces game, retrieves tenderly, has not whined in line and has been under reasonable control. In the US, Show Champions win their titles on a points basis.

When I first became interested in English Springer Spaniels, show dogs could be tested for a Gundog Working Certificate at a field trial, where time was set aside during the trial, usually

The show English Springer is taller and has more feathering than English Springers bred from working lines.

before lunch, for dogs to be tested. As more people became interested in field trials, and the standard of trial dogs improved, it became difficult for the judges to give time to conduct these tests thoroughly. Nowadays some societies organise a show gundog working day where dogs can qualify for the certificate, but there can be little doubt that the standard of work seen at these events cannot be compared to that seen at many gundog working tests.

THE WORKING TYPE

The working Springer has developed as breeders have concentrated on producing dogs with working ability, speed, drive in cover and style, particularly an active back end, including a longer tail than is seen on the show type. Many of these dogs will be smaller than their show counterparts and have shorter ears and less feathering. Any Champions found in this pedigree would be FT Ch. (Field Trial Champion). To achieve this title, a spaniel must have gained two first prizes in Open Stakes at field trials.

A field trial is a competition to assess the work of gundogs in the field. A spaniel trial involves the dogs hunting, finding and flushing game or rabbits for the gun. When game is flushed, the dog must sit, watch it away and then retrieve it tenderly to his owner/handler on command. Such events are licensed by the Kennel Club and are organised by societies registered with and approved by the Kennel Club. Approximately 250 field trials for spaniels are held in a season (i.e. 12 August to 31 January). Kennel Club approved judges officiate at trials for novice or open qualifications.

In addition to winning two firsts in Open Stakes, a dog must successfully complete a water test. The abbreviation FT Ch. is the only KC-recognised award on a working dog's pedigree, although some owners include FTW for Field Trial Winner.

The other KC-approved type of competition for gundogs is a

The working English Springer must have speed, strength and stamina in order to flush out and retrieve game.

gundog working test that seeks, without game being shot, to assess the dog's working abilities. These tests are not as tightly controlled by the Kennel Club as are field trials. They are criticised by the field trial purists, as they do not test a dog as much as a field trial does, particularly for a tender mouth. Hunt tests in America are probably the nearest thing to the English gundog working test. In their hunt tests they have various classes to cover different types of cover and game.

Many of today's handlers find working tests to be a good starting point for gundog competitions, however, and many handlers use them as a useful way to assess a young dog in company. The CLA Game Fair, other game fairs and many country fairs organise gundog working tests as an attraction. I still recall the first time I watched the working tests at the CLA Game Fair; I sat there entranced. Imagine my excitement when, a few years later, I was invited to compete.

It is estimated that over 80 per cent of the English Springer Spaniels now bred are of the working type. I have always had working-type dogs and my first real experience of the different types occurred quite a few years ago at a shoot. Two of us were using our dogs to hunt for a dead partridge – he with his show Springer, and me with my field trial Springer. The ground was very wet and had been grazed over by a herd of cows, which had left many large hoof prints. My dog was flashing about; his was steadily covering the ground. Eventually his dog picked it out of a hoof print and he said his dog had scented it; I said he'd trod on it! Either way, for many years he was delighted to tell me, "Speed is not everything" – and he was right! He had the type of dog to suit him and all I could think was: "Thank the Lord I had the type to suit me."

TEMPERAMENT

There is a considerable variation in the temperament of the show and working types, so prospective

AMERICAN FIELD TRIALS

American Kennel Club (AKC) field trial rules require very similar qualifications for both dogs and judges. The main difference is that one type of field trial is confined to amateur handlers. Titles earned by dogs competing in their trials are:

- FC Field Champion
- AFC Amateur Field Champion
- NFC National Field Champion

There are two additional titles: **DC** Dual Champion for qualifying wins on the show bench and at field trials and **TC** Triple Champion for qualifying wins on the show bench, at field trials and at obedience trials. I would be very surprised if any present-day working-type English Springer could obtain these two qualifications. I cannot see how they could be even entered for a show class as those I have judged and worked successfully in field trials cannot, in any way, comply with the Breed Standard.

Conversely I have not seen a show-type dog that could in any way compete successfully in an Open Field Trial. I remember one handler who was determined that he could train a show-type Springer to win field trials. He produced a well-trained dog lacking the necessary drive or ability to compete successfully. He won a few certificates of merit in novice stakes. I cannot recall anyone with a working-bred Springer even contemplating entering a show.

owners would be advised to meet owners with their dogs, to decide which type would best suit their activities.

The working type is very active; I have heard them described as hyperactive, inquisitive, mischievous, enthusiastic, and wanting to do everything in a hurry, including investigating all different types of cover and smells wherever they may be. The show type, while displaying similar characteristics, is quite prepared to work at a much steadier pace. All English Springers, of either type, should be happy, affectionate dogs that are anxious to please.

Trainability varies in both types of Springer, but I suspect that in general the working type, if allowed to grow up before any restrictive training is started, train on much quicker. I also suspect that a dour type of trainer would be better suited to the bigger somewhat slower show type. The main danger for owners of either type is to mistake enthusiasm for indifference to their owners' requirements, thereby inhibiting the very quality that is the essence of the English Springer Spaniel.

AN IDEAL HOME

A house in the country could be considered ideal for walks, but prospective owners should be aware that the English Springer Spaniel's natural hunting characteristics can create havoc if not properly controlled. English Springers adapt well to town living, providing the owner is willing to take the dog to suitable exercise areas.

I have never kept a dog in the house, working on the theory that a dog requires his own space, which can best be provided by a suitable kennel and run. However, I have to accept

Working tests are a good introduction to the world of working gundogs.

The English Springer is an adaptable breed and will live happily in kennels if he is a working dog, or in a home if he is a companion dog.

that, these days, people expect to keep their animals inside the home. Before doing so, it is important to decide where the boundaries are going to be. Many people do not allow their dogs upstairs or in the bedroom areas, and it may be that there should be at least one room outlawed to any family pet so that you can receive visitors who are anti-dog or perhaps allergic to dog hair.

I was once invited into a house where there were two English Springers in permanent residence. The wife was certainly far from house-proud and dog hair was everywhere. When I see the amount of hair I remove from my kennels, I realise what a problem this could be in the house, so it is vital that the dogs are kept well groomed, especially in the moulting season. Likewise, a Springer will often come into the house wet from his walks or covered in mud, and this, too, must dictate where he is to be kept.

The kitchen and utility areas are those most often chosen to house an indoor dog, and this is usually because there is a washable floor and somewhere convenient to place a box or bed. It is important to remember that the English Springer is a natural thief where food is concerned; he must be trained not to beg at the table and he should not be left on his own with the Sunday roast defrosting invitingly on the work surface! Equally, he should not be encouraged to lie on armchairs or any other bed but his own, and, if he is to make himself comfortable on a cool floor, encourage him somewhere other than in the doorway where you have to step over him! It is far easier to manage a dog that knows what is expected of him so that you and your English Springer can live happily with mutual respect.

EXERCISING SPRINGERS

The English Springer is a very active dog and requires regular exercise if he is to remain fit and healthy. Free-running exercise is, of course, ideal but the dog must be adequately trained. It should be appreciated that the owner needs to walk much further if the dog is tethered to an extending lead. Dogs vary considerably in their requirements. This is particularly true of working dogs during their intensive training period (i.e. starting between six and eight months through to 12 to 14 months). Too much exercise during this period can mean that the dog is not 'fresh' when receiving instruction. Exercise prior to six months should only consist of short walks on the lead and general play in the garden.

It is generally accepted that, once trained, a companion adult Springer requires a minimum daily walk of around an hour, with a combination of walking on the lead and free running. It is important that the dog's natural instincts are catered for, even if he is not to be a gundog, so exercise should include finding and retrieving objects, with lots of praise and encouragement from you. A working dog would be expected to keep going for several hours at a time and, like any athlete, would need his exercise to be built up during the summer until his fitness is at a level to enable him to do this.

Regular exercise combined with mental stimulation should be considered a must for this active breed.

If an English Springer has been correctly reared, he will get on with other dogs – and will tolerate other animals.

ENGLISH SPRINGERS WITH OTHER ANIMALS

Both types of Springer, working and show, get along with other dogs if they are socialised correctly. This is illustrated at dog shows, field trials and gundog working tests where even a growl would cause raised eyebrows. Some dogs may, if being kennelled or expected to occupy a box in a car with another dog, give a few warning growls. This should not be judged to show ill temper; usually the other dog realises that this is just a reminder that liberties should not be taken. Similarly, an older dog, when confronted by a puppy, may quickly show the pup his 'place in the pecking order'. It is as well to be aware of this, as human interference at this time is not usually necessary. If you need to put two adult dogs together in a box/crate or kennel for the first time – particularly if one of the

dogs has used the box/crate regularly – give them some free-running time together first. This usually prevents any problems.

The stronger hunting instinct developed in the working Springer could cause problems with other pets unless introductions are carefully arranged. A lady I know has kept pet cats and Springers all her life, but they still chase other people's cats. She has bred rabbits that she would regularly put on the patio with her dogs, keeping them at Sit while the rabbits hopped about. She tells me that all the dogs wanted to do was wash them! However, it would be unwise to put the average Springer to the test, and dogs should always be supervised when in the presence of small animals.

I have sheep in my paddocks, and I make sure that any youngster or new dog quickly looks away before he can get too

interested. I don't raise my voice often when training or handling, but this is one time that I do. A shout of "No!" and quick movement on my part underlines my dissatisfaction. A few lessons of that type usually means that livestock is safe.

There are numerous dog training clubs, which always welcome new members. Just a word of warning – a Springer's nature does not usually allow him to take kindly to serious obedience training. However, attendance with a young dog of four to eight months old should help him to meet and see other dogs without actually joining in repressive activities. I remember seeing two young spaniels who had received their initial training with retrievers (i.e. walking to heel, sitting etc.) and although they were very well-behaved dogs, they never hunted freely.

The kindly English Springer enjoys the company of children.

If your English Springer is to be a companion pet and you are not planning to train him to work, then I would suggest you follow the training advice given in Chapter Six.

ENGLISH SPRINGERS AND CHILDREN

I cannot recall a Springer who was not happy to accept the company of children, although it should be stressed to any child that respect is two-way. I find that children who are by nature very quiet or nervous in a dog's company and creep about can make mature dogs feel rather uncomfortable and may produce a growl or a bark. The Springer has sensitive hearing and may not appreciate a child screaming or squealing in his presence. It is probably better if a puppy and a child grow up together.

Playing with a young dog is to be encouraged but teasing is definitely not. Some adults cannot resist teasing, but, when they tire of this, they expect the dog to switch off. A woman called to see me a few years ago to ask me what I would do to stop her spaniel biting her children's hands. My reply was that if the dog was biting them, then it should be put down. It then transpired that the dog was being playful, as, every evening when the husband came home, he teased the dog with his handkerchief in his hand. My suggestion was that perhaps she should get rid of her husband or, if that was not possible, she should make sure that the teasing stopped forthwith. The latter, I understand, cured the problem.

TRAINING A GUNDOG

Most Springers, even at eight to 10 weeks old, are natural retrievers, an attribute to be fostered but not over done. I have seen some dogs that, having worked on game, quickly lose interest in canvas dummies. Often, if you could trace their earlier training, you might note that they have been given too many easy retrieves on open land and become bored as a result. Retrieves from cover, long grass, bracken or brambles should be utilised as often as possible, thereby keeping the dog's interest.

One of the best tips I heard, given when a young dog was not interested in canvas dummies, was to put the dummy in the tripe bucket overnight – it worked! Minced raw tripe is easily obtained nowadays, so even if the owner does not feed tripe to his dogs, it would not be a bad idea to buy some tripe and put it in a container overnight with a dummy.

It has been said that there are no bad dogs only bad trainers/handlers. Like most generalisations, this is only partly true. I am firmly of the opinion that bad trainers make bad dogs. For example, a sensitive dog is very unlikely to reach his full potential with a trainer that subjects him to an overly regimented regime. Conversely, an insensitive or hard type of dog will be only too willing to take advantage of a softer type of trainer.

Over the years, due to selective breeding, most Springers are more sensitive and require firm (not hard) training methods, particularly in their early days. Occasionally I am told, "My pup's doing well; he is only three months and he is sitting perfectly." My only reply to that is, "Let's see what he's doing at 12 months."

Sitting (and staying) is the most repressive exercise for a spaniel, and it is one that I do not undertake until the dog is six to eight months old. Walking quietly on a lead and coming back when called is not so repressive, and, in my opinion, is to be preferred in a dog's early months.

With careful and sensitive training, the English Springer will be a first-class worker in the field.

WORKING SPRINGERS

The athletic English Springer is seemingly tireless when working in the field.

An excellent sense of smell, coupled with an eagerness to work, makes the English Springer an ideal sniffer dog.

THE ULTIMATE GUNDOG

The English Springer Spaniel is, in the opinion of many shooting enthusiasts, the maid of all work or the complete gundog. He is required to hunt up game within gunshot and retrieve on command to his handler. This, for the non-shooting reader, means the English Springer Spaniel undertakes his main function, i.e. springing game for the gun, but also undertakes the job of the specialist retriever. To do this he must not only retrieve game he has seen fall, but be directed to an area where game has fallen that he has not seen fall. He must do this without hunting out ground unnecessarily, thereby flushing game out of shot. An English Springer Spaniel can be trained to act as a retriever (i.e. he can sit quietly by his owner while game is being driven over and shot – or missed, as the case may be). At the end of the drive, he can be sent to retrieve whatever game is down. If, during the drive, a bird is shot but not killed, the spaniel can be immediately sent to retrieve, thereby minimising suffering. To undertake these duties the dog requires the ability to scent live, dead and wounded quarry.

WORKING IN OTHER FIELDS

The breed's scenting ability was, no doubt, one of the main

A hearing dog can transform the life of a deaf person.

Stephen Greenhalgh leads a full life with the the help of his disability support dog, Jerry.

qualities recognised when detector or sniffer dogs were being developed to search for drugs and explosives. In addition, the Springer's natural athleticism, agility and enthusiasm made him the first choice for this activity, and he is employed by the armed forces, customs and excise and in the prison service. Most of these dogs are taken from a rescue situation between nine months and two years, and it seems that dogs with a working background, particularly those who have been well socialised and are quite confident in the town or city, are proving most successful. Other sniffing activities include locating arson, cancerous cells in humans, the presence of mobile phones, and even rare newts and bumblebees!

The Springer's natural enthusiasm and trainability make him suitable for assistance dog work, helping people with disabilities, or as a therapy dog, visiting people in hospitals or residential homes. I was pleased to see a smart English Springer called Jaz making the final of the Friends For Life competition at Crufts 2007 with his young owner who suffered from a rare form of epilepsy. Not only could Jaz anticipate a forthcoming seizure, but also his unconditional love and companionship lessened the risk.

THE FIRST ENGLISH SPRINGER SPANIELS

Chapter 2

The history of a breed could justify a book all of its own. However, in this chapter an attempt is made to outline the history as it is known of the English Springer Spaniel and its forefathers. The English Springer Spaniel, as a breed in its own right, has only been in existence since the beginning of the 20th century. However, spaniels can be traced back many hundreds of years and have evolved through a chequered past of different names and much interbreeding.

ORIGINS

Spaniels are thought to have been brought to this country from Spain by the Romans. No one can prove the origin; the name could be derived from 'Hispania', the Latin for 'Spain', or the French word 'espagner', meaning 'to crouch'. There is certainly literary mention of spaniels as far

The traditional role of the English Springer Spaniel was to 'spring' or startle birds for the guns.

back as the 15th century in a number of books. Manuscripts from the reign of Henry IV refer to spaniels springing game for hawks and hounds. We have only to look at famous works of art to see a spaniel featured, and many of them bear an uncanny resemblance to the spaniels of today. However, at this time in history the Springer Spaniel was not a defined breed; it would be another 400 years before it was recognised as a separate breed. From these early beginnings until the late 1880s, all spaniels were working dogs.

There is no doubt that the popularity of the spaniel, both historically and today, is due to its temperament. Whether used as a working dog, show dog or as a family pet, the spaniel has a kind and biddable nature. His willingness to please makes him highly suitable to train for numerous jobs. Before the advent of the English Springer Spaniel,

spaniels, in whatever guise, were trained to flush game. Over the years certain traits became desirable in these dogs, and owners started breeding to 'type', seeking the required characteristics to suit the dog's job of work. In the early history it is clear that most spaniels were used in the hunting field, although smaller spaniels – which were probably the forefathers of the Cavalier King Charles – were developed as 'comforters' as they were called at the time.

During this period, reference is made to a variety of spaniels, such as the Water Spaniel and Cocking Spaniel, names that were obviously derived from the work the dog was doing. In these early years, owners were interbreeding dogs to obtain the required traits, and it is likely that the modern English Springer Spaniel is derived from a number of spaniel breeds and maybe even from setters.

THE EARLY YEARS

Back in the late 18th century the spaniel family was beginning to split into three groups, identified mainly by size and the game they hunted. First the toys, who nowadays are probably Cavaliers; then the two sporting groups: the Cockers for woodcock and smaller game (these dogs weighing up to 25 lb), and above them, the Field Spaniels (a generic term for any working spaniel). Classification was very much by size rather than type, and as a dog grew it could move into another category. This trend continued for many years, although in 1800 the Boughey family founded their strain of Aqualate English Springers and started their own stud book in 1813, predating the Kennel Club recognition by several decades. However, it would appear that none of the Aqualate dogs was ever registered.

Another owner who started keeping his own stud records was Charles Cyril Eversfield of Denne Park, Horsham, whose Denne stud book features pedigrees from 1812 to 1912. Featured in this stud book are two spaniels, Mop and Frisk (owned by Sir Thomas Fenton Fletcher Boughey Bart), who could possibly be credited with being the foundation of the modern-day Springer. An oil painting of Mop, born in 1812, and Fan, 1817, was featured in the *Sporting Magazine* December 1831. This extract shows the high regard in which these dogs were held:

Mop and Frisk: Today's winning Springer Spaniels can be traced back to these dogs.

"That faithful attachment which is proverbial with the spaniel 'Mop', the old dog possessed in the highest degree. This was joined to all those essential qualities which make a spaniel valuable; a good nose, under excellent command, versatile in pursuit and equally good at either woodcock, pheasant, hare, rabbit, snipe or mallard. On land or in water, it was a matter of indifference to Mop which, if it was his master's wish, guided by the hand, checked by the whistle, indefatigable in his labours; his end regretted, being accidentally killed. Frisk, when painted, was young. She possesses a pleasing archness of countenance, which is indicative of bustle and industry, qualities in the spaniel always desirable; both dogs were bred by Sir Thomas."

From these two dogs a line was produced that can be traced through to today's winning Springers. A direct line from Mop and Frisk can be followed via dogs in the Denne stud book, with names such as Fop, Squib, Curley and Fan through to Champion Velox Powder, born in 1903, the year after Kennel Club

SPANIEL CLUBS

In 1859, with the advent of dog shows, the various spaniel breeds began to separate, by size and colour. The Kennel Club was founded in 1873 with its official registrations and stud book, which set the seal on breed definition and separation. In 1885, the Sporting Spaniel Club was founded to arrange competitive matches in the field for hunting spaniels. The first field trial was held on Mr W. Arkwright's Derbyshire estate in January 1895 but, of course, no Springer Spaniel was featured, as the breed would not exist officially until 1902. The English Springer Spaniel as we know it today owes its existence – in the main – to the stalwart working fraternity.

recognition. Besides Mop and Frisk, Velox's pedigree largely consists of dogs with single names, sometimes purely identified by their owner, such as "Fan, 1817 from Warburton's keeper, Bentley, Staffs" or "Paris (Mr Hill's)". Clearly these dogs were highly prized for their working prowess, and could often be identified with the estate on which they worked. Although a force to be reckoned with, the Denne kennel was unfortunately sold up on the premature death at 44 of Mr Eversfield. One of the bitches sold to the Duke of

Hamilton and Brandon was Reva of Avendale (great-granddaughter of Velox) and she in turn produced one of the Dual Champions of the day, Rex of Avendale.

OFFICIAL RECOGNITION

Despite being in existence in one form or another for hundreds of years, the English Springer Spaniel was officially recognised by the Kennel Club in 1902. Now you might think that having been recognised as a separate breed, the rest is history. The truth is very different. Show classifications, although few and far between for the English Springer Spaniel, showed the classes being split into 'over 50 lb' or 'under 50 lb and over 25 lb'. Other classifications were 'English Springer Spaniel other than Clumber or Sussex' or 'English Springer Spaniel (other than Clumber, Sussex or Field) old-fashioned, medium-legged spaniels, any colour'. Wow!

THE FIRST TITLE HOLDERS

July 1903 saw the arrival of Velox Powder, sired by Mr Pratt's Randle and out of Sir T. Boughey's Belle. A direct descendant of Mop and Frisk, after 14 generations, Powder went on to become a Champion, winning in the field and the show ring. The first Challenge Certificate (CC) awarded was at Crystal

INFLUENTIAL SPRINGERS

Velox Powder: A Champion, winning in both the show ring and the field.

Rivington Sam: The first English Springer Spaniel Field Trial Champion.

Palace in October 1903, judged by Mr W. Arkwright, who gave the CC to Beechgrove Will from the smaller size category; this dog was the son of two unregistered Field Spaniels. In bitches, the CC went to Fansome, who was by Punch ex Beechgrove Chrissy, and a great-great-granddaughter of an 'of Ware' bitch; she won a total of three CCs between 1902 and 1904. Beechgrove Will was made up at his next two shows and became the first ever English Springer Champion.

Although much of the breeding of English Springer Spaniels was from working and show stock combined, it was not until 1913 that Rivington

Sam became the first Field Trial Champion. Sam's dam was an over-sized Cocker Spaniel called Rivington Riband; his sire was Spot of Hagley. The practice of mating between different spaniel breeds continued for many years and may account for the different colours that were registered at the time. Stud book records show many various colours, including blue and black; liver roan; lemon and white; and golden, liver and white (some tri-colour that one!). Another interesting fact is the mating of unregistered dogs with registered dogs, some being quite prolific winners, something that is undesirable today, as the

progeny would not be eligible for Kennel Club registration.

Up until this point in time, dogs could be shown or trialled and in either case gain the title of Champion, but in 1909 the title of Field Trial Champion (FT Ch.) was approved by the Kennel Club. By 1914 and the start of the First Word War, only nine Springers had become Champions. The Championship show scene did not start again until late 1920 with the Scottish Kennel Club, where Little Brand won the dog CC and Horsford Honeybell won the bitch ticket.

DUAL-PURPOSE SPRINGERS
The year 1921 saw the founding of The English Springer Club,

FT Ch. Bee of Blair: A great worker in the field and an influential dam.

FT Ch. Style O'Vara: One of 17 Champions produced by the O'Vara kennel.

making it the oldest and senior breed club. By 1924 there were approximately 15 Championship shows classifying English Springers. Needless to say, the working fraternity continued as best they could during the war, and many of the top winners of these years were the result of matings between show and working Springers. In fact, many Springers achieved great success in field trials and on the bench. In the same year, Mr R.R. Kelland, who had been training his field trial dogs since the turn of the century, joined The ESS Club and served as Secretary, Chairman and President over a 30-year period.

Around this time, Mr G. Clark's Blair kennel was very successful in the field. FT Ch. Bee of Blair was not only highly successful in the field, she also proved a good dam, producing many field trial winners. Mr Selwyn Jones and Mr T.J. Greatorex were responsible for making up 17 Champions for the O'Vara kennel, including FT Ch. Scramble of O'Vara, who won the Kennel Club Spaniels Championships twice. The Pinehawk kennel was also a successful working kennel in the 1930s.

In the early part of the 20th century, owners and breeders still regarded their dogs as dual purpose, putting them in the show ring and regularly shooting over them. The breed produced three Dual Champions: Horsford Hetman, Flint of Avendale and Thoughtful of Harting. Famous affixes and influences in the early years were: Avendale, Beechgrove, Tissington, Horsford, Velox, Denne, Laverstoke and Rivington. Registrations, understandably, fluctuated a great deal during the two wars, but prominent prefixes in the 1920s were Beauchief (Mr F. Warner Hill), a direct line from Champion Little Brand; Marmion (Hon George Scott); Solway (Mr Grierson); of Ware (Mr H.S. Lloyd); Shotton (Mr M. Withers) and Ranscombe (Dorothy Moorland Hooper).

Ch. Dry Toast: His bloodlines were behind many winning Springers.

Ch. Higham Tom Tit: A fine representative of the breed, combining show and working lines.

Top winners were Ch. Winning Number of Solway, Ch. Dry Toast and Int. Ch. Showman of Shotton who had considerable influence both here and later in America. Ch. Jess of Shelcot and Ch. Beauchief Barham were also in Mr Withers' kennel, which was managed by the famous Mrs Gwen Broadley. Miss C.M. Francis and her Higham prefix will be remembered for her efforts to bring the working and show lines together; her best-known dogs were Champions Higham Teal, Topsy and Tom Tit, owned by Lady Lambe.

Just after the outbreak of the Second World War, two dogs were the top winners and had considerable influence on the breed. These were Ch. Pleasant Peter and his son, Peter's Benefactor. No Championship shows were held during the war period and so Peter's Benefactor – while winning many awards – never gained his title.

POST-WAR SPRINGERS
The English Springer Spaniel Club held its first post-war show in 1946. It was at this time that Joe Braddon began a winning streak with Starshine of Ide and Ch. Invader of Ide. Mrs Gwen Broadley was also prominent at this time with her Sandylands prefix, as was Mr Hepplewhite with the Happeedaze suffix. In field trials, Harpersbrook, Criffel and Staxigoe were prominent kennels.

THE BREED SPLITS
At this time the breed began to divide between the 'show' and the 'field trial' type. Many people will say that this was the beginning of the end of the truly dual-purpose English Springer Spaniel. The intervening years have seen a divergence of type between those who prefer to work their dogs and those who show them. Working English Springers are now generally smaller than their 'show cousins', have shorter ears, lighter bone and considerably less feathering.

The early 1950s continued successfully for the above-mentioned kennels but others began to appear, most notably that of Ernest Froggatt (Moorcliff). The Moorcliff kennel produced several Champions, including Ch. Moorcliff Dougal of Truelindale, who went on to sire Ch. Hawkhill Connaught. Mrs Smithson of the Studley kennels had success by using Boxer of Bramhope to

Ch. Alexander Stubham:
A son of the great Boxer,
and an influential stud
dog in his own right.

Bountiful of Beechfield, producing Champions Studley Major and Brave Buccaneer, as well as Am. Ch. Studley Hercules in successive litters in 1952, 1953 and 1954. Bountiful was also mated to Banker of Bramhope, which resulted in Ch. Studley Diadem and Debutante. Studley Major, when mated to Debutante, then produced Sh. Ch. Studley Oscar in 1959. Mrs F. Till's Alexander of Stubham (son of Boxer) won his first CC in 1951 and became a leading stud dog. Many notable breeders came on to the scene at this time including: Sandy Davies (Colmaris) with the two litter brothers, Sh. Ch. Colmaris Ranger, winner of 11 CCs, and Mr D.C. Hannah's Sh. Ch. Colmaris Bonny Ladd, who won 14 CCs; Mr Hannah also bred

BOXER'S INFLUENCE

By the end of the 1940s a young stud dog called Boxer of Bramhope was having an outstanding influence on the breed, and many cite him as the greatest Springer of all time. The Bramhope kennel, owned by Mrs Mary Scott, produced many winners but it could be said that the main influence was through the sons of Boxer. These were Champions Clintonhouse George, Peter of Lorton Fell, Studley Major and Alexander of Stubham.

Having said this, Boxer is directly responsible, on both the sire and dam's side, for Show Champion Hawkhill Connaught and Champion Mompesson Remember Me, two dogs that went on to hold the breed Championship record. Mrs Scott saw the need for an outcross and imported two dogs from America – Am. Ch. Melilotus Shooting Star and Am. Ch. Dr Primrose of Wakefield – but they did not prove to be popular stud dogs in this country.

FIELD TRIAL CHAMPIONS

Major Spittle, who was Field Trial Secretary of The ESS Club, bred Dinas Dewi Sele, a field trial Champion that was among many handled by Keith Earlson. The Markdown affix of Mr F. Thomas was highly successful in the 1960s; is probably best known for FT Ch. Markdown Muffin, who was trained and handled by John McQueen. Mr McQueen then moved to the Rytex kennel, another famous trials kennel that produced – among many – FT Ch. Rytex Rex in 1969. Later in the decade, Harry Hardwicke, at one time Chairman of both the Kennel Club Field Trial Committee and the Spaniel Club, owned and trained FT Ch. Lewstan Paul, the first of ten field trial Champions he has produced. Tim Healey produced three field trial Champions between 1970 and 1975 under the Farway affix.

Other notable kennels were Jonkit, Hamers and Saightons, all of which have had a strong influence in America. Other trainers of note during this period were Rachel Gosling with her Park Maple Springers and, in Scotland, two names that stand out were Billy Bremner and Danny Mackenzie (Staxigoe). Lawton Evans won the Spaniel Championship on four occasions, first with his own bitch, Coppicewood Carla in 1971, twice with Sport of Roffey in 1975 and 1976, and once with Cleo of Coppicewood in 1978, both owned by David Cock, Chairman of the Field Trial Committee at the Kennel Club. Ian Openshaw moved to the Rytex kennel after John McQueen, handling first for Fairfax Naylor and then for himself – in the 1980s and 1990s he produced more than 30 FT Champions.

The breed has divided, and dual-purpose English Springers are very rare.

Show Champions Stokely Bonny Boy, Gay Boy and Lucky; Mrs I. Sherwood (Sh. Ch. Woodbay Prima Donna and Ch. Woodbay Gay Charmer); Mrs Ellen Dobson, who owned the outstanding bitch of her time Sh. Ch. Teesview Pandora of Truelindale, sired by Ch. Teesview Titus, and Mrs Judith Hancock of the famous Hawkhill kennel.

Up until this time, an English Springer Spaniel could be either a Champion on the bench or a field trial Champion. The Kennel Club then introduced the title of Show Champion in 1958 for those dogs that had won three Challenge Certificates in the show ring, and they could gain the title of Champion if they gained the Gundog Working Certificate. The Kennel Club's decision to create the separate titles probably was the final nail in the coffin for truly dual-purpose Springer Spaniels. After this time the 'split' in the breed became very evident, and it is extremely rare to see a 'working' bred Springer in the show ring and vice versa, although there are some stalwarts in the breed who maintain the working element with their show dogs, regularly shooting over them in the winter season.

THE GREAT CONNAUGHT

It was in the era of the late 1960s and 1970s that the great Sh. Ch. Hawkhill Connaught, who was bred by Judith Hancock and owned in partnership with Jimmy Cudworth, dominated the show

The great Sh. Ch. Hawkhill Connaught.

scene; he is remembered by many of today's exhibitors, who can trace their own dogs directly back to him. The breed record holder for so many years, he was only surpassed by Ch. Mompesson Remember Me in the 1990s and subsequently by Sh. Ch. Wadeson Inspector Wexford in 2005.

Connaught was born on 11 July 1969 and was by Ch. Moorcliff Dougal of Trulindale out of Sh. Ch. Slayleigh Paulina,

both big winners in their time. 'Con' won his first CC at the tender age of 13 months and proceeded to carve a name for himself by winning 14 more, 13 with Best of Breed out of the 25 sets of CCs on offer in 1971. He also won the Gundog Group on three occasions (Paignton, Cardiff and Southern Counties) with two Reserve Groups at Leicester and Richmond. In 1972 he gained a further 14 CCs, all with Best of Breed and including Crufts, from the 25 sets of CCs on offer that year. He won seven Best in Show awards at general Championship shows, the Gundog Group at Leicester, and Reserve Group at Birmingham National and Southern Counties. Not surprisingly, he became Dog of the Year all breeds. In 1973 he won a further 13 CCs with BOB and, as his owner judged Crufts that year, Con couldn't go. However, he won Best in Show at Bath, Chester, Darlington and National Gundog, with Group wins at Birmingham National and Reserves at Windsor, Paignton, Bournemouth and Belfast, and was once again Dog of the Year all breeds.

Con went to Crufts in 1974 and won the Gundog Group. He also picked up another CC at Leeds. By now Con was running out of judges to go under (as Jimmy and Judith had made the decision not to show him under the same judges at breed level), and so he was only lightly shown. Although this decision was respected, it probably denied Con the opportunity to continue winning in both Group and Best in Show rings.

Sh. Ch. Hawkhill Connaught left his mark in the ring where his record of seven Best in Show and 17 Gundog Group wins at general Championship shows remains unbeaten. He will also be remembered as a great sire. Con sired 25 Champions, a record that still stands today. These 25 and five other ticket winners won 154 CCs between them. A grandson, Sh. Ch. Graftonbury Genghis Khan, was a top winner and popular stud dog in the 1970s and 1980s. He won a total of 25 CCs, four of which were at Crufts.

He won a Reserve Best in Show at a general Championship show and three Groups, including the Gundog Group at Crufts in 1985.

INFLUENTIAL KENNELS
The Cleavehill kennel has been very influential on the breed, and with black and whites in particular, especially during the 1970s, 1980s and 1990s. There have been at least 27 English Show Champions bred by the late Jean Taylor (there may be more and, if so, the author apologises), and Cleavehill Champions are to be found in Europe and Australia. Probably the most important Cleavehill litter was born in 1972, sired by Sh. Ch. Hawkhill Connaught out of Cleavehill Skye Maid. This produced three Show Champion littermates: Tartan Arrow, Tartan Banner and Tartan Special.

Ch Swallowtail of Shipden: An outstanding black and white Springer, winner of 18 CCs.

REMEMBER ME

It was on on 13 November 1986 that Mompesson Remember Me, bred by Bob and Francis Jackson, was born. She was sired by Sh. Ch. Hawkhill Starsky out of Mompesson Country Girl. She won her first CC in 1988 at the age of 19 months from the novice class at Border Union. 'Jill' made 1989 a year to remember by winning 17 CCs; she also finished Top Gundog that year. In 1990 she won another eight CCs, six with Best of Breed. She was then withdrawn from the show ring towards the end of the year for her impending litter to kennelmate Sh. Ch. Mompesson Dream Chaser. On her return to the ring in 1991, she picked up another five tickets, four with Best of Breed including Best in Show at the English Springer Spaniel Club Show.

In 1992, Jill won another nine CCs, six with Best of Breed, and became the bitch record holder when she won her 36th CC at the Scottish Kennel Club show. In 1993 she again took some time out to have her second litter of eight puppies. One of these pups, Sh. Ch. Mompesson Memory Lane, went to Ann Corbett (Trimere) and in turn produced another top winner in Sh. Ch. Trimere Time to Remember from Mompesson. Jill won another five CCs that year, four with Best of Breed. Another momentous occasion took place in 1992 when she gained her Working Certificate and became a full Champion at the age of seven!

As a veteran in 1994, Remember Me went on to win eight more CCs, seven with Best of Breed, and then broke Connaught's long-standing CC record by winning her 51st CC at the East of England. Jill's last litter was born 30 December that year, and she had nine lovely puppies. Maternal duties kept her out of the ring until early 1995 when she came back and won a further two CCs, both with Best of Breed. In her career, Jill won a total of 55 CCs and had earned herself a place in the record book; she subsequently retired to the armchair, where she remained Francis' adored pet until she died in 2000.

Sh. Ch. Mompresson Remember Me: She had a stunning show record, and also produced 25 Champions.

Colin and Carolyn Muirhead have been tireless in their campaigning of dual-purpose Springers under the Shipden affix. They have produced six Champions, three of which took their full title. Colin and Carolyn are also well known for their black and white Springers, with Ch. Swallowtail of Shipden probably being the most well known. Notable liver and whites from this kennel were: Sh. Ch. Persimmon of Shipden, Sh. Ch. Ir. Ch. Sotherton of Shipden, Ch. Aus. Ch. Bomaris Envoy to Shipden and Sh. Ch. Shipden Chuck Berry. The kennel's latest Champion is Mistily's Magic Merlin to Shipden, who is a Swedish import. Other kennels that have had an influence on the black and white Springer include Lady Lambe's Higham kennel (Lady Lambe was a member of William Arkwright's family and he arranged the first ever spaniel field trial), and Ian and Olga Hampton's Larkstoke kennel.

The Feorlig kennel owes its existence to Don and Jenny Miller's introduction to the breed by Morag Bolton (Pencloe) and in particular a litter of puppies that contained future Champions Pencloe Driftwood and Dynamo. The Millers' first Springer was an Easter present from Morag, and the Feorlig affix came about because Don and Jenny honeymooned at Feorlig House on the Isle of Skye. It was in only their second litter that they produced Sh. Ch. Feorlig Beautiful Memory, Feorlig Breakaway (1 CC) and Feorlig Bannerman (1 CC). This first great success was followed by a number of Champions including Feorlig Golden Griffin, Feorlig Golden Gayle and – probably their most successful dog – Sh. Ch. Feorlig Van Der Valk, who achieved 14 CCs. Although she never became a Champion, Feorlig Jus' Jolene became the foundation bitch for the Wadeson kennel.

Jan Wood originally used her Ardencote affix to register Labradors, but in 1973 she started in English Springers with Hawkhill Tranquility. Mated to her grandfather Hawkhill Connaught, Tranquility produced Sh. Ch. Ardencote Tapestry, who won 12 CCs and was top-

Sh. Ch. Feorlig Beautiful Memory, owned and bred by Jenny and Don Miller.

THE WADESON STORY

Another kennel that started in the mid 1970s is the Wadeson kennel of Colin and Kay Woodward. Little did they know when they obtained their first Springer in 1975 that they were destined for greater things. Bitten by the showing bug after obtaining a well-bred pet Springer, they chose their next puppy because it had the straightest coat! This turned out to be Barlochan Engineer, who became their first Show Champion. A foundation bitch from the Feorlig kennel, F Just Jolene was the next step and the rest, as they say, is history. They have bred several Show Champions including Wadeson Shoestring, Juliet Bravo, The Equalizer, Jessica Fletcher and Miss Marple. Despite the disadvantage of competing directly against Remember Me, Sh. Ch. Wadeson Miss Marple won a total of 32 CCs, 22 RCCs and two groups, as well as RBIS at WELKS. 'Jennifer' will always be remembered for the special smile she gave everyone and her permanently wagging tail.

Wadeson Ruth Rendell, mated to Sh. Ch. Speeton Seafarer, was to produce the outstanding Sh. Ch. Wadeson Inspector Wexford on 1 September 1995. Winning his first Challenge Certificate at 13 months and doing the 'double' on the day with Sh. Ch. Wadeson Jessica Fletcher, the second certificate swiftly followed. 'Sinbad' became a Show Champion at 18 months, winning his third CC at Crufts together with Gundog Group 3. He went on to win a total of 61 CCs, 50 of which were achieved with BOB, with the last won at nine years old. He also had two all breeds BIS, two RBIS and six group wins at general Championship shows and won the 'Pedigree Chum Pick of the Litter Award' as well. This tally surpassed Mompesson Remember Me and made Sinbad the breed record holder. He has sired five Show Champions to date but, sadly, died in 2007 aged $11^1/2$ years. He will always hold a very special place in Colin and Kay's hearts. Colin and Kay are immensely proud of Sinbad and agree that all his awards were special, but, of course, they are especially proud of the breed record.

Sh. Ch. Wadeson Inspector Wexford: Breed record holder with a tally of 61 Challenge Certificates.

winning ESS bitch in 1978 and 1979. A repeat mating produced Sh. Ch. Ardencote Autosport. The kennel has also bred South Afr. Ch. Ardencote Adventurer, Sh. Ch. Ardencote August Love and Ch. Ardencote Alexander, who was originally sold as a pet but went back to Jan because he was too lively!

Mr and Mrs Doug Sheppard's kennel started in 1973 with Silveroak Elaine, who, when mated to Ch. Teesview Titus, produced Ch. Cliffhill Juliet and Ch. Cliffhill Julius. The Sheppards were always keen on the working side and gaining their dogs' Qualifying Certificates. Many dogs were exported and gained their titles, among them Swed/ Int. Ch.

Cliffhill Gossips Field Day.

Mrs Margaret Bower enjoyed considerable success with her Bowswood Springers and she bred many Show Champions, including Ch. Bowswood Barleycorn and Ch. Bowswood Botany Bay, and owned Ch. Woodgill Shadowfax of Bowswood, who gained her Qualifying Certificate at eight and a half years old.

INTO THE 21ST CENTURY

Although this book cannot do justice to the many people involved in the breeding and showing of English Springer Spaniels today, recognition must be given to those people who, having started out in the 20th century, are still continuing very

successfully in the breed today. Two kennels that have already been mentioned are Mompesson and Calvdale. These two highly successful kennels have been at the forefront of the show scene now for a number of years. They, among others, are bearing the fruit of their carefully considered breeding programmes to produce consistently good stock that has won well here and abroad. The use of their stud dogs has also proved influential upon the breed.

MOMPESSON SPRINGERS

Bob and Frances Jackson have kept English Springer Spaniels at the forefront of the show world and every year sees at least a couple of new Show Champions crowned as well as winning such accolades as 'top sire in the breed'. Frances' love for the breed was founded at the Hawkhill kennel where she was a frequent visitor from the age of six. At 10 years old, she was given her first English Springer by Judith Hancock, Hawkhill Derby Daydream, who went on to become a Show Champion and foundation for the Mompesson kennel. Mated to Mary Scott's Sh. Ch. Lochardils Ghillie of Bramhope, she produced Sh. Ch. Mompesson Midsummer Dream and Int. Ch. Mompesson Fisherman. A second litter by Ch. Swallowtail of Shipden produced Mompesson Midnight Cowboy, who became a Scandinavian Champion and the bitch Mompesson Sleeping Partner, which Frances gave to Judith. Judith campaigned her to

Sh. Ch. Mistily's Magic Merlin to Shipden: The first imported, undocked English Springer to gain his title.

her title and she was then sold to Australia. Due to family commitments, Frances did not show a lot during the 1970s but came back with Sh. Ch. Raenstar Country Boy of Mompesson, who sired three Champions in one litter. One of these was Sh. Ch. Mompesson Pride and Joy, the grandsire of Remember Me.

CALVDALE SPRINGERS

Frequently competing against the Jacksons, Nicola Calvert's Calvdale kennel has been consistently successful. Some of the most notable dogs owned by Nicola include Sh. Ch. Windydale Whimsicle Ways of Calvdale, Ch. Black Ebony of Burmon at Calvdale and Sh. Ch. Skilleigh Tan Sandy. In more recent years the kennel has produced a number of Champions, including her latest Show Champions Calvdale Call Off the Search, Calvdale Claire Blake and Calvdale Softly Softly. This tradition is being continued in the family through Nicola's daughter, who also successfully campaigns her own dogs.

A GREAT TRADITION

Starting back in the 15th century through to 1812 with Mop and Frisk and on to three outstanding dogs who became breed record holders and finishing with many well-respected, successful kennels, it is clear that the English Springer Spaniel is a popular and well-loved breed. In the intervening years, there have been many a great dog and many a great breeder – too many dogs

and significant breeders to mention. Some of the leading names (but by no means all of them) during this time include Moorcliff, Stubham, Teesview, Tyneview and more recently Ardencote, Eastriding, Graftonbury, Lyndora, Roandew, Robil, Trimere and Wadeson.

It is in no way intended to be disrespectful to those not mentioned nor to their contribution made to the English Springer Spaniel – only lack of space prevents their inclusion. To do justice to the history of the English Springer Spaniel, the breed we all love, requires more time and space than this publication can offer.

Annual registrations for the English Springer Spaniel are now over 15,000; a minority of these – around 2,000 – come from show-bred lines. It is fairly safe to say that there may well be an equal number of unregistered puppies produced annually still displaying the enduring qualities that were recognised by our ancestors and which make the English Springer Spaniel the wonderful companion that it is.

THE ENGLISH SPRINGER SPANIEL IN AMERICA

It has already been mentioned that Mrs Mary Scott imported two Springers from America but little has been mentioned of the Springers that were exported from their homeland to America and what influence they had there. Although there was some

Ch. Springbok of Ware, bred by Mr H.S. Lloyd in the UK and exported to the USA.

Ch. Showman of Shotton: He became a British, American and Canadian Champion.

movement of Springers to America before this, the first one to be registered with the American Kennel Club was Denne Lucy in 1910. It wasn't until 1922 that the American Field Trial Association was set up and the following year saw the first show that classified English Springer Spaniels, held at Maddison Gardens. Canadian Ch. Springbok of Ware was purchased from the famous Mr H.S. Lloyd and he had a great influence on the breed in the USA. He was a dog that still typified the dual-purpose Springer that was the norm at this time.

INFLUENTIAL IMPORTS

English Springer Spaniel kennels were starting to be established and Ch. Nuthill Dignity, another import, became an American Champion. The first ESS to become a bench Champion in America was Horsford Highness, a daughter of UK Dual Ch. Horsford Hetman. Fifteen other Horsford dogs won their bench

titles over a four-year period. Many dogs were imported from the Scottish kennel of the Duke of Hamilton under the Avendale affix. One such dog was Dual Ch. Flint of Avendale, who was exported to the similarly named Avandale Kennel in Canada and Rex of Avendale was the grandsire of UK/Am. Ch. Rufton Recorder. Progeny of Ch. Rufton Recorder were exported and later followed by their sire, who became an American Champion at the age of eight. Champion Showman of Shotton added his American and Canadian titles to his name when imported by Paul Quay.

Lady Portal exported Laverstoke Powder Horn (who became an American and Canadian Champion) and UK Champions Laverstoke Pepper and Pattern along with numerous other Laverstoke dogs to Henry Shaw to establish his own kennel in Vermont, using the same prefix. The Clarion kennel, established in 1924, imported Rufton Dinah, Tandy, Ruler and Roger, who all became

Champions. The latter sired Dual Champion Fast and Ch. Clarion Trumpet, both of whom became Best of Breed winners at Westminster. The Horsford, Rufton, and O'Vara kennels were all very influential on the breed in America. The Camden kennel, which bred field trial Springers, was based on Rivington and O'Vara lines.

The Second World War caused the reduction in imports from the UK and many American owners did not continue in the breed after the cessation of war.

SALILYN SPRINGERS

Probably one of the most well-known ESS kennels in America is that of the late Mrs Julie Gasow whose Salilyn affix has enjoyed great success. Starting in the 1930s and continuing well through the 20th century, this kennel's most influential dog was Am. Ch. Salilyn's Aristocrat who sired 188 Champions. This dog's pedigree can be traced back to the Rufton, Shotton and Beauchief kennels in England.

In the late 1970s another of her top-winning dogs was Am. Ch. Salilyn's Hallmark, whose great-grandmother was Am. Ch. Kennersleigh Cleavehill Beliza Bee, which was imported from the UK. She was the first bitch to be made up in the USA since the war and was bred by Jean Taylor. Among the Champions bred by Mrs Gasow are Salilyn's MacDuff, Classic, Hallmark and Major Domino, to mention but a few. This kennel has been very influential on a number of other kennels in the USA.

LEADING BREEDERS
Other breeders who have gained success in the American show scene are Andrea Glassford (Jester); Anne Pope (Filicia based on Melilotus); and Francie Nelson (formerly Chuzzlewit now Fanfare). Finally, coming right up to 2007 is Ch. Felicity's Diamond Jim, who won BIS at the Westminster Kennel Club Show. James is owned by Teresa and Alan Paton, Ruth Dehmel and Diana Hadsall and was bred by Teresa and Ruth. His handler, Kellie Fitzgerald, won the same award with another Springer in 2000. James is by Am. Ch. Telltale Davey Jones ex Embur Autumntime Rendition. This breeding is highly influenced by the Salilyn kennel and consequently can be traced back to the UK kennels.

There is no doubt that the English Springer Spaniel in America looks vastly different to those dogs from its original homeland. This seems to be a

Am. Ch Salilyn Condor: American-bred Springers now have a distinct look that sets them apart from their British ancestors.

fairly modern change, as photos of dogs in the 1970s still appear to retain their 'Englishness'. The American dog show fraternity are renowned for their unique grooming and showmanship and this has led to their English Springers being groomed differently to their English counterparts. Whether that is the only difference or whether there has been a divergence between

the two countries, such as happened with the working and show Springer, is a matter of opinion.

Again, there may be many kennels not mentioned in this section that have been active participants in the English Springer Spaniel in America. Their contribution will always be recognised in the pedigrees of modern dogs.

AN ENGLISH SPRINGER FOR YOUR LIFESTYLE

3 Chapter

I would like to think that anybody deciding on having a dog these days would be much more knowledgeable than was possible when I acquired my first English Springer Spaniel 25 years ago. I was fortunate to grow up in a 'doggy' household and had met many a Springer Spaniel when I was beating on shoots as a child, but my family had never owned one. I fell in love with the exuberance and the look of the breed, and the rest I learned as I went along.

Today, we must accept the responsibility that comes with dog ownership. We have to do our homework. There are several ways of tackling it.

MAKING THE COMMITMENT

First and foremost, is this the breed for you? Can you cope with a lively yet biddable dog that will need exercise, training, mental stimulation, grooming, and much affection from you? Are you prepared for mucky paws, wet ears, moulting, a constantly wagging tail, and a dog that is a natural thief and can easily reach a kitchen worktop?

WHO WILL LOOK AFTER YOUR DOG?

In today's world, most people need to work, be it full- or part-time. This does not necessarily preclude ownership of an English Springer. However, it has to be managed well and thought through carefully.

Some people may work from home. Some may be able to take the dog to a place of work. However, the average person will rely either on a partner or parent who is living with them to fill in the gaps away from home, or they will have to consider engaging the services of a reliable, professional dog walker or sitter to look after the needs of the dog in their absence. This does not come cheap and must be added to the projected costs of dog ownership, such as food, training classes, minor veterinary bills, insurance premiums, kennelling, and visits to the grooming parlour.

Consider also that a puppy will require a greater input of time, with up to four meals a day required initially to fulfil his growth potential. House training and basic obedience are also a must, and it is essential that a puppy is not bored or he will turn his attention to destruction. I have heard of Springers munching their way through three-piece suites, the kitchen floor, wall and doors, and other expensive items because the dogs were left on their own for long periods of time.

Taking on an English Springer Spaniel will affect the whole family.

HOW MUCH DOES IT COST?

Many people wishing to own a purebred dog decide to take on a puppy. The actual cost of buying a puppy will vary hugely, depending on whether it is from unregistered parents with no papers, or from top field trial or show-bred litters. It is wise to check the sort of money you can expect to pay with a breed club secretary. I remember a pair of 11-week-old puppies I fostered for our breed rescue society that, three weeks earlier, had cost one-and-a-half times more per puppy than the show-quality litter I had just sold, and, although they were sweet-natured, they were not from health-tested stock nor from winning parents of either type.

In addition to the initial purchase costs, there are the on-going maintenance costs of dog ownership. A few years ago a well-known charity estimated the annual cost of keeping a dog to be in the region of £400 per year, and this will have risen considerably since. The expected lifespan of an English Springer is approximately 13 years and can be a great deal more. I know of at least three who have hit the 17 mark! Over the course of a dog's lifetime, these maintenance costs can be considerable, and deserve closer examination.

FEED

What to feed your English Springer is a question of choice and is explained further in

40

Chapter 5. However, your Springer's dietary requirements add up to a considerable sum over the year and can be doubled during the shooting season if he is to be a working gundog.

EQUIPMENT

Although every dog needs some essential items – such as a bed and bedding, collar and lead, food and water bowls, some grooming tools, and a constant supply of 'poo bags' – these can be very basic and need not break the bank. A collapsible crate for travelling and house training is very helpful and worth every penny of the additional cost.

TRAINING

There is nothing worse than an untrained Springer Spaniel. How far you progress with training is entirely up to you and depends largely on the activities you wish to pursue with your dog. However, it is essential that your dog receives a certain level of basic obedience training even if he is kept purely as a pet.

There are excellent training clubs that offer courses in puppy socialisation, basic obedience, competitive obedience, heelwork to music, and agility (see Chapter 6), in addition to the Kennel Club's Good Citizen bronze, silver and gold award scheme. Many gundog societies hold group sessions for training to the gun or can direct you to an expert who will train you and your dog on an individual basis. If you are interested in showing your puppy, most general canine societies offer ringcraft classes (in which you will be taught how to present your dog to its best advantage) on a weekly basis with a competitive match show monthly to get you both

Whatever the weather, a Springer needs lots of physical exercise coupled with mental stimulation.

COPING WITH HOLIDAYS

If you cannot take your Springer on holiday with you, you will need to make arrangements for your dog's care while you are away. There are three choices here, the first being the boarding kennel, the second being home boarding, and the third being pet/house sitting.

BOARDING KENNELS: Most kennels advertise in local telephone directories, and your local veterinary surgeon will keep a list. Your vet may also have details of individuals who would be happy to care for your dog in their own home.

If you choose to board your dog in kennels, it is important that you see the kennel well in advance of booking a stay. You should ensure that the accommodation offered is – in your opinion – of a standard suitable for your dog, that there are adequate exercise facilities, and that the dog's dietary and bedding needs will be met. Costs can vary considerably, and it is worth remembering that it may be just as expensive to pop your dog into a quality kennel for a fortnight as it is for the return airfare to an exotic holiday location!

All kennels will expect your dog to be fully vaccinated and up-to-date with boosters (within the previous 12 months), and staff will ask for a certificate as proof. While in its care, the dog will be covered by the kennel's own insurance and you should inform your own insurance company if your animal is being looked after elsewhere. However, if your dog requires veterinary attention or grooming during his stay, these costs may well be extra, so you should check this in advance.

If the dog is still a puppy, it may be that your puppy's breeder will be happy to provide accommodation, and this is another question to ask when viewing a litter. The advantages of this arrangement are that it is likely to be less stressful for your puppy, as the breeder's dogs and home are already known to him, and, of course, the breeder will recognise all your puppy's little idiosyncrasies. Some breeders will board your dog at any time if they have the facilities, but most will charge a fee to do this.

HOME BOARDING: This is where the dog goes to stay in someone's house and has to fit in with other dogs in a family situation. This option can work very

into shape. Fees for these courses are generally modest although you can expect to pay much more for individual training and for the advice of a corrective behaviourist should you take on an adult dog with problems. For details of all these societies, individual trainers, and behaviourists, contact the Kennel Club or a breed club secretary.

MINOR VETERINARY BILLS
There are certain routine visits to the veterinary surgeon that are unavoidable and are unlikely to be covered by the average insurance policy, such as primary vaccination and annual boosters, neutering, pregnancy, whelping and euthanasia. Some vets also charge a consultation fee for routine flea treatment and worming advice, although

most will incorporate this in your annual booster visit.

Most vets offer a microchipping service. If the dog's breeder has not microchipped the dog, you should consider doing so, as permanently identified dogs are a deterrent to dog 'nappers' and very helpful to the local authorities responsible should your dog get lost or stray.

well if your dog is well socialised and enjoys the company of other dogs.

HOUSE SITTING: This is where someone stays in your own home to look after the dog. This is particularly useful and cost effective if you have several pets, and it also has the added advantage that the house is not left empty. Some house sitters will even water your houseplants for you. Your vet may be able to recommend house sitters or you can contact a reputable pet-sitting company.

Shared holidays with a Springer are a great bonus, but if you can't take your dog with you, you will need to make other arrangements.

INSURANCE

This is an absolute must for anyone who owns a dog, and, on an annual basis, it can cost 25 per cent of your initial purchase price. Apart from covering third-party liability should your animal cause an accident or damage, it will also pick up the tab for major veterinary bills. In addition, many policies will pay for kennelling if an owner is hospitalised or incapacitated. However, it is important to remember that the policy will have an excess built in that will be deducted from your claim, and this means that some smaller veterinary costs will have to be paid by you in any event.

GROOMING

If you do not have the time to do this yourself (and it is not difficult), contact your breeder, who may well be happy to do this for you or may recommend an expert in your area to trim your English Springer to a high standard. Hand-stripping a spaniel's coat is surprisingly expensive, as it can take many hours. Alternatively, your vet or local pet shop will have details of grooming parlours and mobile groomers who will tackle your dog's coat in your own home. It is not expensive to build up some basic tools to keep the dog clean and tidy but remember that neutering a dog can affect the texture of the coat and may result in a great deal more work and even the need to take off the coat with electric clippers.

THE RIGHT PUPPY

Before you start your search for a puppy ask yourself if you want your English Springer to be simply a pet, a working gundog, or a show dog. A pet can be either working-bred or from show stock. You need to decide whether you would prefer to buy one from a Kennel Club registered litter rather than one without papers. Both will probably have typical characteristics of the breed, but with a registered litter you know exactly what dogs are behind your puppy's breeding. This is important should you want to breed a litter yourself in the future, or if you plan to use your dog at stud if he is successful in your chosen discipline. It is not possible for an unregistered dog to participate in Kennel Club field trial working tests nor will it be permitted to enter an Open or Championship pedigree dog show.

WORKING OR SHOW?

There are visible differences between working dogs and show stock, which can be easily seen by looking on any of the breed websites. In short, the working dog can be smaller, with finer bone, shorter and higher-set ears, and less feathering; his head will have a broader, flatter top to the skull, and his muzzle may well be less square than his 'show' counterpart. If you want an English Springer as a pet, you should choose whichever type you find most aesthetically pleasing. Both types come in liver and white, black and white, or either of these with tan markings. The most popular colour is liver and white, but I have a really soft spot for the black and white, and dogs of this colouring have a distinct advantage in that their coats rarely bleach in direct sunlight, so less work is required on the grooming table!

If you would like to work your

A Springer from show lines will need more regular grooming, as it has more feathering than a working Springer.

ENGLISH SPRINGER COLOURS

Liver and white.

Black and white.

Black and white with tan markings.

Liver and white with tan markings.

dog, you will be looking for a sire and dam that are worked to the gun, and their pedigrees will probably contain a good spread of field trial-winning dogs that have proven their ability to do this in competition. Some show-bred dogs have retained their ability to equip themselves well in the field, but, on the whole, they work at a slower pace and are not suitable for competition. Likewise, the working dog usually will not fare well in the show ring, as he is not bred purely for conformation, but for speed and intelligence.

A breed club secretary will point you in the right direction for the type of dog you prefer, but remember there is never a guarantee that either type will excel and that your training and handling will play as great a part - as will an element of good fortune.

DOG OR BITCH?

This is a very hard question. I usually suggest that potential owners choose the puppy whose looks and character most appeal to them, then turn it over to find out what sex it is. I started with a bitch because my family had always had bitches. It was three generations on that I kept my first dog puppy. What a very special dog he turned out to be. He rapidly became my favourite and his loss was the hardest to bear.

Generally speaking, the dog puppy will grow bigger than the bitch, and is, therefore, heavier and stronger. If unneutered, he can be a little harder to manage when his hormones kick in at around seven months, and he will need firmer handling as a 'teenager'. He may urinate more frequently in public spaces, leaving his 'mark' as a warning to other male dogs, and, if his

testosterone levels are high, he may be less friendly than is the norm should he meet another dog with similar masculinity. On the plus side, he is likely to be devoted to you, very eager to please, and a real character.

The bitch is lighter in build, generally less wilful and she is said to be more biddable. However, she can be prone to mood swings dictated by her hormones, and her coat is likely to moult more as her season approaches – generally twice a year. It is unlikely that the characteristics of either sex will be affected in any way by neutering.

Single dogs are unlikely to be a problem – dog or bitch – but there are obvious complications if you keep more than one entire dog of both sexes! I have known households where several male dogs live in total harmony, and I have kept bitches together for

English Springers are sociable dogs and will live peacefully together in mixed sex groups.

years without any disagreements. These days I have separate facilities for both my dogs and bitches when the need arises, but all my dogs live together as one big, happy family at other times.

FINDING A BREEDER

It is wise to contact a breed club secretary, who will ask you what type of dog you most prefer and will then put you in touch with the club's puppy-line manager or the secretary of the field trial section for that club. Alternatively, you can obtain a list of litters registered in the previous three months direct from the Kennel Club or its website. The American Kennel Club runs a similar service on its website (see Appendices).

The breeder may have a website with photographs of the litter, its dam and sire and other dogs in his kennel. Check this out. If the breeder is on the internet, ask to see photos of the available puppies. If you are happy with what you see, make an appointment to view the litter at the earliest time allowed (usually around four weeks of age).

VIEWING THE LITTER

If you have very young children, it may be a good idea to leave them with a friend on your first visit, as children can be very persuasive and you need to be

QUESTIONS TO ASK

Regardless of how you find a breeder, you should have a list of questions to ask so that you can satisfy yourself that you have as much knowledge as possible before you view a litter, particularly if you are having to travel some distance to do so.

- Is the litter Kennel Club registered?
- Is the litter from working or show stock?
- How many puppies are available for sale and what size was the litter?
- How old are they and when would they be ready to leave?
- What sex are they?
- What colour are they?
- How are the dam and sire bred, and are they available to view? (Most people use outside stud dogs so ask to see a photograph of the sire if possible.)
- Are the puppies home-reared or kennel-reared, and would you be able to see their accommodation? My puppies are born in the kitchen and stay there for the first four weeks. Sometimes, depending on the weather, I

transfer them to a kennel so that they can enjoy the sunshine in an outdoor run. If it is a small litter, they usually stay in the house. Home-rearing is preferable, for a pup's development, but, in or out, the important aspect is that they are well socialised, have plenty of hands-on attention, and are kept in clean conditions.

- Have the sire and dam been tested clear for hereditary eye diseases and canine fucosidosis (see Chapter 8). Ask for documentary proof of this. Has either parent been hip scored? If the answer is yes, ask to see the certificates; the lower the scores the better.
- Are the puppies to be sold fully or partly vaccinated, and is this included in the price?
- Will the breeder microchip the puppies before they leave, and, again, is this included in the price?
- Ask the price!
- Will the breeder offer life-long advice for the dog, and will he or she take the dog back if you need to rehome the dog for any reason in the future?

English Springer puppies are hard to resist, but try not to let your heart rule your head.

reasonably objective on the initial visit. On a follow-up visit, or when you come to collect your puppy, it is important for both you and the breeder to see how the children interact with the dogs and puppies so that you can lay down the ground rules before taking on the responsibility of a young dog and equally young children.

Arrive as near to your appointment time as possible and, if you are held up en route, let the breeder know. You will probably meet (and hear!) the adult dog(s) first. If the puppies are very young, the mother may be a little protective, but she should soon settle. Look carefully at any other dogs there to satisfy yourself that they have the temperament you are looking for. Remember that the puppies may be very sleepy if they have been

fed recently. Their personalities are not very obvious at four weeks, but you should establish that they are nicely rounded, bonny babies, worth a second look. At around six weeks, they should be quite playful and happy to come to you to be picked up. This is definitely the best time to choose, and you will probably be attracted to a particular puppy by its character or markings.

Discuss with the breeder what activity you would be interested in doing with the puppy, and the breeder will help you identify the one who shows most promise. For working or showing you will need to find a puppy that is confident but responsive, and may already be showing signs of being happy to retrieve a small toy or can be stood foursquare on a table by the breeder to

demonstrate his potential for the show ring. You may just want a quality pet, so do not settle for any puppy with which you are not totally captivated!

GETTING TO KNOW THE BREEDER

You will have had the opportunity to discuss many aspects of owning an English Springer with the breeder and he will ask a number of questions about you and your lifestyle to be sure that this is the breed for you. By the end of your first visit you should feel that you could contact him at any time with any worries you may have and establish that he would take the puppy back if some disaster were to befall you and you were no longer able to keep the doog.

If you are happy with your choice, the breeder will probably ask you to leave a percentage of the purchase price as a deposit, with the balance payable when you return to collect the puppy once he is at least eight weeks old.

CHOOSING AN OLDER DOG

Not everyone wants a puppy and the upheaval that his arrival can cause. My first English Springer was an adult, aged two, and she soon became a much-loved member of the family. She remained with us for nine years until, sadly, she died from cancer. However, we were very fortunate to breed two litters from her and she is behind all our current stock. Taking on an older dog can be just as rewarding and enjoyable as purchasing a puppy.

I would advise you to consider all the questions you would ask if you were choosing a puppy. You should satisfy yourself that the adult dog has been well looked after, has the necessary documentation, and, above all, is a healthy, well-adjusted animal.

You can buy an adult working dog that is already trained to the gun, but you would be wise to see it in action, or in conditions resembling those found on a shoot, before you buy. Dogs such as these are sometimes advertised for sale in the shooting press, or you may hear of one available through the field trial secretary of one of the breed clubs. Beware buying a 'partly trained' gundog, however; as a friend once remarked: you can never be sure exactly which part of the dog has

been trained! A fully trained dog is an expensive option and you must spend time allowing him to settle before you can expect him to want to work for you.

Similarly, you can achieve instant success in the show ring by taking on a successful dog from another kennel, although you have to allow time to build a harmonious relationship with the dog.

CHOOSING AN ADULT

You have several options when choosing an adult dog as a pet. Some breeders may have 'run-on' a puppy, hoping that he will develop into a successful working or show dog. When this does not happen, and because of the limitations on the number of dogs a breeder can keep, the

It is important to see the mother with her puppies, as this will give some indication of the temperament they will inherit.

A rescued dog often needs rehoming through no fault of his own.

breeder may decide to find him a caring home as a pet. Most will inform their breed club secretary and it is worth checking with the secretary to see if they have any young, adult dogs on their books.

Some breeders will have adult dogs that cannot be bred from. For example, a bitch may have suffered a womb infection and been spayed, or a dog may not get along with other dogs in the household. Again, the breeder will advise the secretary and these dogs would make excellent pets whatever their age.

Dogs purchased as adults from breeders can cost anything from something very modest to far more than you would pay for a puppy, so always check in advance.

If you buy an adult dog from a breeder, it is possible that the dog may have been kept in kennels and may not be house trained. This would be one of the first questions you might wish to ask. On the plus side, most of these dogs will be well trained otherwise, used to the company of other dogs, and accustomed to being groomed. I can assure you that, being a Springer, a dog such as this will love you from the moment you start feeding him and taking him for walks, but, like all dogs, he will not feel totally settled for a period of up to three months after arriving at your home.

RESCUED DOGS

Your final option is to take in a rescued dog. The popularity of the breed has resulted in a considerable number of English Springers requiring new homes due to a whole host of compelling reasons, from broken homes and the death of an owner, to the family that takes on this breed without thinking of the needs of such an exuberant character and simply cannot cope.

FINDING A RESCUED DOG

There are several breed rescue charities, all of which do a great job in trying to find the best available home for the Springers in their care. A breed club

Be patient as your Springer settles into his new home and learns what you expect of him.

secretary or your local vet will also have details of these charities and help you to find your nearest rescue co-ordinator. It is also worth checking with the major general rescue charities, as many English Springers pass through their doors. Most of the charities concerned have a website, some of which have details of dogs available for adoption and have downloads of the form for potential adoptees and details of where to send them.

YOUR NEW DOG

The English Springer Spaniel is now the third most popular family pet in the UK according to official registration figures released from the Kennel Club. In America, the breed ranks as the 26th most popular. This is, in itself, testament to the breed's endearing qualities as a companion. Regardless of whether you take on an adult Springer or a puppy, or breed one yourself, with the right care you are guaranteed a friend for life.

THE NEW ARRIVAL

Chapter 4

Excitement! After carefully considering the pros and cons of taking on an English Springer Spaniel, the decision has been made to introduce a new addition to the family. You can liken the experience to having a new baby, or, in the case of a rescued dog, an older child. It is vitally important that you are thoroughly prepared for your new arrival, not only for the dog's safety and happiness, but also to ensure that the transition period is as smooth and stress-free as possible for the owners.

Most of the factors given here are meant with a puppy in mind, but they apply equally to an older dog. The extra considerations that must be given to an older, rescued dog are discussed later in the chapter.

GARDEN SAFETY

Starting outside, the new owner must walk around the garden, assessing any dangers. The garden gate is often a weak spot. Look at this and check that the gate is near enough to the ground to prevent a puppy from passing underneath. Also check that it is high enough to stop a dog from jumping over to explore the other side. Bear in mind that a fully grown dog may easily scale a gate that bars a puppy's access perfectly well – think ahead. If the gate is made from wrought

An English Springer pup is a great explorer, so you will need to check out your garden for potential hazards.

POISONOUS PLANTS

It is important to check that no cocoa shell mulch is present in your garden, as this can cause illness, or even death, when eaten. Also check all your plants, as some are harmful if ingested. Puppies tend to think they are helping you do your gardening by chewing your beloved plants or digging holes (never where you want them to dig, of course). Some of the most common dangerous house and garden plants are amaryllis bulbs, asparagus fern, azalea, cyclamen, daffodil bulbs, day lilies, delphiniums, foxgloves, hemlock, hyacinth, hydrangea, ivy, laburnum, lilies, lily of the valley, lupins, mistletoe, morning glory, nightshade, oleander, poinsettia, rhododendron, rhubarb leaves, sweet pea, tulip bulbs, umbrella plant, wisteria, yew, and some berries, mushrooms and toadstools. If your dog chews or eats any of these, seek veterinary advice immediately.

iron, you will probably need to mesh the lower part to make sure that your puppy cannot squeeze through. Also check all your garden boundaries, paying particular attention to gaps between the bottom of fencing and the ground. Make sure a puppy cannot squeeze underneath.

You may need to put up guards to protect your puppy from other garden hazards, such as pools, ponds, and steep drops at the edges of patios or lawns. Check your garden shed and garage for dangerous substances, such as weed killer, slug pellets and rat baits. Ensure that these products are kept on a high shelf, just in case a determined puppy is able to gain entry.

TOILETING AREA

You may want to cordon off an area that your puppy can use as a toilet area. The site should be positioned fairly near the house but away from children's play areas. It is quite easy to train your puppy to use this designated toileting area simply by leading the dog to the area every time you take him outside to relieve himself. The main points to remember are always to take your puppy to the same area when he needs to relieve himself, and to make sure this is at regular and frequent intervals, such as after sleeping, eating, and every couple of hours otherwise. One tip I give new owners is that, if the breeder has reared your puppy on shavings, buy a bag of shavings and sprinkle some in the

Allocate an area of your garden for toileting, and your pup will quickly learn what is required.

Try to see your home from a puppy's perspective, and this will help you to spot possible dangers.

designated spot, changing it regularly. However, be aware that some dogs may refuse to go on anything other than the surface they are used to in their designated area. For this reason, it is important to teach your dog to eliminate on other surfaces as well.

It is vital to pick up faeces from your garden. Not only is it very unpleasant to step on faeces accidentally when they have been left lying around, but it is also a potential health hazard. Removing faeces will prevent any possible worm infections that may affect you, the children or reinfect the puppy. Should your designated area be on concrete or paving stones, you have the advantage of being able to hose down the area regularly with disinfectant. Check with your local authority to see if it has a special waste disposal site for bagged faeces.

SAFETY IN THE HOME

Houses are designed for people, not animals, and they contain lots of hidden hazards for your puppy. One of the best ways to check each room – although it may make you feel very silly – is to go around on all fours. Assessing the room at this level allows you to see what is within reach of an inquisitive, playful puppy. Exposed electrical cables are particularly dangerous, especially in hidden corners. Chewing quietly in an out-of-sight corner is great fun for the puppy, but it can be fatal for the dog and very costly for the owner.

Stairs are a definite no-go area for your puppy. Not only are they

55

dangerous should your puppy fall, but going up and down stairs is also very bad for your pup's growing bones. One of the easiest solutions is to buy a baby/stairgate until such time as your puppy knows his boundaries.

In some ways, puppy-proofing your home is not dissimilar to toddler-proofing. Lock away all medicines, cleaning products and dangerous chemicals; remove from reach any objects that could cut your puppy or cause him to choke; and ensure that you keep all chocolate, cocoa powder, raisins, grapes and macadamia nuts shut away, as these are poisonous to dogs. Use your common sense – and, if in doubt, play safe.

HOME PROTECTION

When I see prospective customers who have children, I take it on myself to give the youngsters a direct chat on tidiness (it always comes better from me than from the parents). Usually, the parents are delighted. I tell the children that they must learn to put their shoes and all their toys out of the puppy's reach. I explain to them that a puppy loves to chew trainers, and, if they have a named brand, how upset they would be to have a big chunk

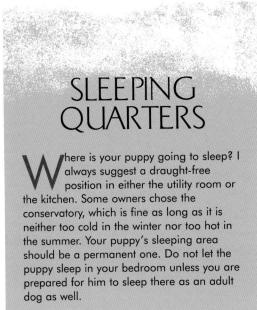

SLEEPING QUARTERS

Where is your puppy going to sleep? I always suggest a draught-free position in either the utility room or the kitchen. Some owners chose the conservatory, which is fine as long as it is neither too cold in the winter nor too hot in the summer. Your puppy's sleeping area should be a permanent one. Do not let the puppy sleep in your bedroom unless you are prepared for him to sleep there as an adult dog as well.

chewed out of one of them. Toys are an even bigger hazard, especially small bits and pieces, such as Lego. These must be cleared away, as, if left lying around and picked up by a puppy, they can cause death by choking. Games consoles are another big issue. Puppies love to chew the wires and carry the controls around. Children must learn to put them out of reach after they have finished playing with them. If children begin putting things away from the time they first come to view a litter until they return to take the puppy home, they have usually had a few weeks to practise their new regime before it becomes vital for the new puppy's safety.

A further problem for new owners who also own a cat, is

cat food. If the cat is normally fed on the floor, a new spot will have to be found. Puppies love cat food but it is not good for them. Find an accessible shelf or surface out of the puppy's reach, and accustom your cat to her new eating area prior to the puppy's arrival.

BUYING EQUIPMENT

Welcoming the new puppy into your home not only involves a new set of responsibilities but also requires you to make sure that your puppy has all the necessary equipment he needs to make the transition as stress-free as possible.

GREAT CRATES

I prefer the puppy to sleep in a crate. A crate is not a cage and using one does not mean you keep your dog locked up. Used correctly, the crate becomes a 'safe haven' for your puppy, somewhere he will feel content and secure and always be happy to go. The crate should be viewed as a special space for your pet, and children should be taught that it is the dog's space and should not be used as their playhouse.

Using a crate has many advantages. It is easier to house train a puppy in a crate, as puppies hate to soil their bed areas. It also means you can confine your dog for short periods while you leave the house

A crate can be used as sleeping quarters or at times when you cannot supervise your puppy.

You can also set up another bed in the sitting room so your puppy can spend more time with you.

or are occupied in another room. You can enjoy peace of mind, knowing that nothing can be soiled or destroyed and that the puppy is comfortable, safe, and not developing any bad habits (i.e. chewing your kitchen units).

A crate is doubly useful in that it can be taken with you when necessary. Your puppy can travel safely in the car if kept in a crate (it is a legal requirement that dogs travel safely so that they are not a distraction to the driver), and, should you be involved in an accident, a puppy in a crate has a much better chance of avoiding injury than an unrestrained dog. Furthermore, a crate prevents your dog from leaping out of the car when the door is opened.

You should buy a crate that is the right size for your dog when he is fully grown. You can always bulk up with extra bedding at first so that your puppy feels secure. You may also want to consider placing a piece of removable plywood on top of the crate in order to use this as a daily grooming area.

Set up the crate with warm, comfy bedding and a heavy, non-tip bowl of water. You may want to line the floor with newspaper to mop up any water spillage and the occasional 'accident'. Most puppies love to curl up on a piece of fleecy veterinary-type bedding or something similar. This is very hygienic and can be washed easily. It is non-allergenic and fairly resistant to chewing.

Get a large piece and cut it into two – one for the crate and one for the wash.

Initially, leave the crate door open so that the puppy can come and go as he pleases. Then, over time, accustom the puppy to having the door shut for short periods of time. Eventually, you will be able to leave your dog in his crate for extended periods of time, although never more than four hours maximum.

Once the puppy is getting to adult age, you may prefer to change the crate for a regular bed, making sure this is always big enough for your dog to stretch out in. There are many different styles to choose from and to suit every budget.

IDENTIFICATION

In the UK it is a legal requirement that a dog carries a visible form of identification. This can take the form of ID tags, carrying the owner's name, address and telephone number, attached to the dog's collar. You can either have these details inscribed on discs, or you write the information on paper and enclose it in a little barrel that is attached to the collar. I prefer the engraved disc to the barrel type, as there is less risk of the details becoming illegible over time. In America, the dog must carry the owner's details, the dog licence details, and a current rabies tag.

A more permanent form of ID is microchipping or tattooing. Most people opt for the microchipping option, as it is cheaper and the details can be easily updated should you move, etc. Be aware, however, that even if your dog is microchipped, if he is found without any visible form of ID, you may still be fined up to £5,000.

FEEDING BOWLS

There are many feeding and drinking bowls on the market, and it is largely a matter of personal choice. I tend to use stainless steel bowls, as these are easier to keep clean. However, some people prefer heavy ceramic bowls, particularly for water, as these are less likely to get knocked and spill the contents all over the floor. Avoid plastic bowls, as most puppies cannot resist chewing them.

You will need two bowls – one for water (make sure fresh water is available at all times) and one for food. A travelling non-spill water bowl is also a big help.

COLLAR AND LEAD

Your puppy will go through several collars as he grows. Whatever style you choose, the collar should be comfortable, and checked regularly to ensure that it fits properly and that the fastening is secure. A collar should not be too loose so that it can slip over your puppy's head, nor so tight that you cannot slip two fingers underneath. If

choosing between a buckled collar and a 'clip' type collar, consider that the clip variety has the advantage that the puppy can be released from the collar very quickly – if it becomes snagged on a branch and the pup starts choking, for example.

Leads are also a matter of personal choice, but they should be neither too long nor too short. Chain leads may be too heavy and are only as strong as the weakest chain in the link. Beware nylon leads, too, as although these are relatively inexpensive and attractive, they can be uncomfortable for your hand. Should you want to do some gundog training, you will also require a slip lead.

GROOMING EQUIPMENT

There is a vast range of grooming equipment available, but spending your money on a small number of high-quality, basic tools is the best option. Start off with the essentials for daily grooming, which are a soft bristle brush, a comb, a slicker. You will also need to buy some nail-clippers, a toothbrush, and some 'doggy' toothpaste.

I would also recommend buying a cheap, battery-operated toothbrush (available cheaply in discount shops). This is not for your English Springer's teeth but so that your puppy can get used to the noise in readiness for when it experiences clippers. I use this on the top of the ears, over the body, and under the feet – areas where the dog is the most ticklish.

Grooming should be done daily. Start as soon as you bring your puppy home, as the earlier he becomes accustomed to grooming, the easier the task becomes. (For information on grooming, see Chapter Five.)

TOYS

Toys are an essential part of a puppy's kit. Toys should be neither too small nor too big and heavy. A tennis ball is good to start him retrieving. Chew toys also provide mental stimulation and help to keep your dog's teeth clean. There is an extensive range of 'kongs' for different ages. Soft toys are also widely available for dogs. A selection of toys that you can play with interactively, such as Frisbees or rubber rings, can make life extra fun.

Tug ropes are popular toys for dogs. However, I advise you strongly not to play with your puppy with these, as a young dog's jaw line does not stop growing and moving until 18 months of age. A cold carrot from the fridge is a good idea to give your puppy while he is teething.

Whatever toys you buy, treat them with the same caution as you would when buying toys for small children. Make sure that there are no loose parts that could come off and lodge in your puppy's throat. Pay particular attention to the stitching on soft toys, as a determined puppy can work loose stitching until the toy splits apart. If this happens, and the puppy ingests the stuffing, the results can be fatal.

FOOD

The subject of diet will be covered in depth in the following chapter. However, you need to

English Springers love to play, and there is a huge variety of toys to choose from.

have a supply of food for your puppy before you bring him home. Check with the breeder what food your puppy is being fed. Most breeders will supply enough food for the first few meals.

Make sure you buy the same food and keep to the same routine as the breeder, as this will be less stressful for the puppy and will avoid upset stomachs. Should you wish to change your puppy's food, do so gradually. Begin by adding a small quantity of the new food to the existing type and gradually increase the ratio over the course of several days until your puppy is eating meals entirely of the new food.

For the first few days, make sure that you give your puppy boiled, cold water. After three days, start to add a bit of cold tap water to each bowlful until you are giving all tap water. The reason for this is that one of the commonest causes of puppies' upset tummies is that, when they go to a new home, the water is slightly different from where they were born.

POO BAGS

Poo bags are an essential item on your shopping list as well. You are required by law to clear up after your dog in public areas and to dispose of the bag in an appropriate bin. You can buy poo

SHOPPING LIST

To summarise, the following is a list of items that should be on your initial shopping list. Buy these items before you collect your puppy, so that you are prepared from the moment he arrives in your home.
- Cage/crate
- Bed and bedding
- Feeding bowls (x 2)
- Travel water bowl
- Collar and lead
- Toys
- Grooming equipment
- Healthy training treats
- Food (on the advice of the breeder)
- Poo bags

bags from any pet store, although it is often cheaper to use baby nappy sacks, and there is no reason why you cannot use any type of plastic bag, including carrier bags (though beware of holes in the bag's bottom!).

FINDING A VET

If you have obtained your puppy locally, your pup's breeder may be able to recommend a vet. Alternatively, personal recommendation from dog-owning friends is one of the best ways to find a veterinarian. It is a good idea to ask people who you meet in the street when walking their dogs which vet they use.

Always visit the vet's surgery

before making a final decision. The premises should be clean and the staff friendly. Make a point of finding out whether an appointment system is used or whether it is a case of first come, first served. Also find out what cover is provided in emergencies that happen outside opening hours. It is a legal requirement for vets in the UK to provide out-of-hours cover. Some vets may offer an on-call service provided by their own vets. Others may have a locum. In America, some practices use the services of a local animal hospital for out-of-hours emergencies.

Once you have decided on a vet, register your puppy in advance. In the case of a puppy, he might need his first inoculations, so book an appointment for a few days after his arrival (giving a settling-in period first). Your puppy's breeder should give you a vaccination record (if appropriate) and details of when your puppy was last wormed. Your vet will need to know these details so that routine worming and flea treatments can be planned. Your vet will also be able to microchip your puppy.

COLLECTING YOUR PUPPY
At last, the day you have been preparing for has arrived and it is time to collect your English Springer Spaniel. Make sure you

After weeks of careful rearing, it is time for the puppies to go to their new homes.

pre-arrange a time with the breeder – the earlier in the day that your pup is collected, the better. This will allow you to be home early, giving your new puppy lots of time in his new surroundings before bedtime.

Make sure you take an old towel, newspaper, kitchen roll, a bottle of your cold, boiled water and a small drinking bowl. Some breeders will give you a piece of bedding from the whelping box, so that your puppy can be comforted by the familiar smell of his mother and littermates. Alternatively, a week or so before collecting your puppy, give the breeder a piece of the bedding that you have bought for your puppy and ask him to put it in with the litter.

When you arrive to collect the puppy, you will first need to sort out the paperwork with the breeder. You should be given the Kennel Club registration certificate, a pedigree, the receipt, a feeding plan, and a list of any medications used (if any). The breeder will also give information about the make of worming liquid/tablets given, and the dates, in order for you to inform your vet and continue with the programme. Some breeders may provide you with free insurance for the first few weeks of the puppy's new life with you. Make sure you have the correct food and any further information that the breeder supplies. Before leaving, confirm with the breeder that, should you need any further information in the future, he will be there to help you.

Most cars have split seats in the back, so drop one seat down and position your crate there. This will allow room for one passenger to sit beside the cage to reassure the puppy during travel.

MEETING THE FAMILY

The day you bring your new puppy home is, of course, a very exciting one. However, never lose sight of the fact that, however wonderful the moment is for you, it will be overwhelming for your puppy. Although everyone will want to meet the new arrival, try to keep introductions limited to

immediate family for the first few days. Ask other members of the family and friends to be patient a little longer and explain that you want to give your new puppy a settling-in period first.

You want to make your puppy's transition away from his siblings as easy as possible. Bring the puppy in to the house calmly and quietly. If children are at home, make them wait calmly until you have introduced your new puppy to his new surroundings. One of the first things you will need to do, especially if you have had to travel some distance, is take the puppy to his toilet area. Next, show your puppy his sleeping area or crate. Offer the puppy a drink, and only then introduce the puppy to the children. It helps if everyone sits on the floor, as this will be less intimidating for the puppy. Get the children to stroke the puppy gently. Never let young children

pick up a puppy, and do not let the children run around, squealing in delight, as this will make the puppy nervous.

Once your puppy has had a chance to see his immediate surroundings, relieve himself, and meet the family, he will want to explore further. Puppies are naturally curious, but, to begin with, let your puppy explore only the areas you want him to spend time in. After a short period of exploration, give your puppy his meal, take him outside to the toilet once again, and then let him rest. If he falls asleep on someone's lap or on the floor, gently lift him into the crate, so that he knows where his bed is.

After a few days, you can introduce your puppy to neighbours, friends and family, making sure you take things slowly and do not include too many at any one time. If you do

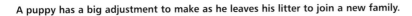

A puppy has a big adjustment to make as he leaves his litter to join a new family.

Given time, an English Springer and a cat will learn to live in harmony.

not have children, invite a friend, relative or neighbour with sensible children to visit, so that the puppy gets used to them.

While it is important to socialise your puppy with other dogs, make sure that your puppy does not meet any other dogs until he has received his full course of vaccinations.

PETS WELCOME

If you have any other pets, introduce them to your puppy slowly. If you have another, older dog, remember that he was there before the puppy, and, until now,

your home has been the sole domain of your older dog. Introduce dog and puppy in as neutral an area as possible. Always supervise their interaction until their relationship is reliable and they get on well. Normally, a young puppy will be naturally submissive to the older dog. The adjustment will not happen overnight, but provided that the rest of the human 'pack' also respect the pecking order – giving attention first to the older dog and then to the new puppy – relations usually settle down quite quickly.

Never introduce dogs at meal times. Each pet must have his own food and water bowls, and the older dog should always be fed first. Each dog should also have his own bed, toys and space.

To introduce a cat to the new puppy, it is best to put the puppy in his crate and then let the cat into the room to sniff the new addition. Once the cat has accepted this, you can introduce the puppy to the cat with the puppy on his lead. Always let the cat have an escape route if she becomes unhappy at any point.

THE FIRST NIGHT

Hopefully, you have got through the first few hours without too much trauma. It is time for bed and everyone is exhausted. Make sure your new puppy has been taken out for a last chance to relieve himself, and then take him to his bed. Put the puppy to bed with a (pet-safe) teddy bear to cuddle up to. Leave a radio on playing quietly in the background and turn off the light. Your puppy may cry for a short while, but this will be because he is missing his mother and siblings. It is best to leave the puppy alone, as he will eventually fall asleep through exhaustion. Do not run to comfort the puppy initially, as you will set up a situation where the puppy cries for comfort constantly.

Should the crying become distressed, you have the same options as a mother with a new baby. Some people believe in letting the puppy 'cry it out' until he becomes used to falling asleep by himself. The premise behind this is that reassurance will teach the puppy that, if he cries, he will receive attention, so he will cry all the more. Other people believe that ignoring an obviously distressed puppy is cruel, and they prefer to reassure the puppy with gentle stroking until he falls asleep, and then sneak quietly away. Both methods seem to work, and the choice you make will depend on your personal feelings and the puppy's character. Whichever option you choose, be prepared to see it through for several days until the puppy has accepted the new regime.

Establish house rules at an early stage – or you might live to regret it!

Your puppy has to be taught not to chase the cat, so reward the pup every time he behaves calmly around the cat. In effect, you are trying to teach the puppy to ignore the cat, so that the cat learns not to fear the puppy. Cat and puppy may learn simply to tolerate each other, but, over time, many become good friends.

In the case of rabbits, guinea pigs, chickens, gerbils, rats and hamsters, the transition can be a little more difficult, as your puppy's chase instinct will be strong, and small pets are more likely to try to run away or hide – just the reaction to encourage the chase instinct. Make it clear that these pets are not your puppy's toys. With the animals safely confined, and your puppy on a lead, take the pup to their cages and let him sniff. Reward him every time he ignores the animals and behaves calmly. Do not let your puppy bark at them, and do not take any risks by allowing your English Springer access to them – the results could be fatal.

HOUSE RULES

I feel that it is important to establish a routine as soon as your puppy arrives. Meal times should be set at regular intervals, as should walks. It is also vital to implement some basic house rules, and this applies to the human members of the household, as well as the dog.

Before the puppy is brought home, shut all gates and doors, especially the stairgate, put shoes away, and tidy all toys out of an inquisitive puppy's reach.

Before the pup joins your family, everyone in the house should sit down and discuss the puppy's training. It is important that all family members use the same commands during training, so that the puppy knows exactly what is required of him. Consistency is all-important. Even young children can be taught the puppy's needs for basic commands. One way to do this, prior to the puppy's arrival, is to have re-enactments using soft toys.

Once you have decided on what commands you are going to use, put the words up on the fridge, using magnetic letters, for the children to read. Young children must be taught that a puppy is like a baby – they need rest and should not be disturbed

when sleeping. Too much play can overtire a puppy and be detrimental to his health.

HOUSE TRAINING

Whoever gets up first in the household must take the puppy out for toileting straight away (even before the kettle gets put on). Toileting should be done regularly, remembering that a puppy needs to go as soon as he wakes up, after he has eaten, after play times, and every hour or two otherwise. Never chastise your puppy for making a mess unless you have caught him in the act. A displeased-sounding voice is quite sufficient. Never resort to old-fashioned methods, such as

rubbing the puppy's nose in the mess. This will not teach your puppy anything other than to fear you. It is far better for your puppy to learn to toilet outside through positive, reward-based methods. Whenever you take your puppy outside for toileting, repeat a special phrase, such as "Go wee" or "Be busy", and lavish the pup with praise for going outside. A few accidents are inevitable, but if you take your pup out regularly, and you are vigilant in watching for the signs that he needs to go – circling and sniffing the ground, for example – a puppy will be successfully house trained in a very short time.

Exercise should be limited while a puppy is growing.

An older dog will need time to settle into a new home.

PUPPY EXERCISE

Once your puppy has had his inoculations, you can start to take him out on a collar and lead. Begin with very short walks initially, building up to longer ones over time. Do not go on long walks, even if your puppy is on a lead. You do not want to damage your pup's growing bones.

Introduce your puppy to traffic slowly. It is a good idea to go to the end of your road and make your puppy sit, just to listen to the traffic, reassuring the dog all the time. Take your pup in the car to a school, attach his lead and wait outside when the children are coming out. Your new pet will get lots of attention, which will help him to realise that new people and new situations are good fun.

Socialisation is vital, so introduce your puppy to as many situations as possible – markets, busy high streets, pushchairs, bicycles, horses (if possible) and water. Do so gradually so that your puppy is not overwhelmed, and always have your puppy on a collar and lead until he is reliable in unfamiliar environments and will come when called (see Chapter 6). Never let your puppy run free before he is six months old (minimum).

TAKING ON AN OLDER DOG

Much of the advice for introducing an older or rescued dog to your household is the same as for a puppy. Just like a puppy, an older dog will feel a little apprehensive arriving at his new home. Whereas a puppy may make the adjustment within a matter of days, be prepared for this to take longer with an older dog – sometimes up to several weeks. Even the most well-adjusted English Springer will need time to feel at home. During this settling-in period, your dog will need lots of patience, love, and not too much excitement. Resist the temptation to show off your new addition to all your friends and relations, as your dog will find the attention of the immediate family more than enough to be going on with at first. Let the dog come to you when he is ready and remember that, just like us, a dog needs peace and quiet for part of the day at least. As with a puppy, show your older dog his sleeping area as soon as you bring him home, and encourage him to use it during the day. It is a good idea

to sit beside the dog's new bed or crate, stroking your new pet gently and using plenty of words of encouragement, so that he understands that this is a 'good' space.

Introduce all new situations and people gradually, and be prepared for things to take time. Check your home and garden for safety, just as you would a puppy. Bear in mind that a fully grown dog, particularly one that may not have been taught basic good manners, may be able to wreak far more havoc than a puppy, as well as being able to reach things out of a puppy's level. It is a good idea to keep kitchen work surfaces free from items you do not want your dog to get hold of. Initially, your new spaniel might be inquisitive and spend a lot of time on his hind legs, especially in the kitchen. Remember that a

spaniel has a great sense of smell and leaving the Sunday joint on the side in his reach is not a good idea.

FEEDING
Hopefully, you will have discussed your adult dog's current diet with the previous owners or rescue centre staff, and it is wise to continue with this diet if it is a sensible one and the dog seems healthy. Should you wish to make changes, this should be done gradually, as explained above when changing a puppy's diet. Do not worry unduly if the dog does not want to eat for the first day or two. This may be due to the dog adjusting to his new environment, and he will begin to eat again once he feels more settled. If the lack of interest in food continues beyond a couple

TRAINING STRATEGY

Many older dogs are well trained and in need of new homes through no fault of their own (such as a family break-up, etc). Others have received little socialisation and training. Be prepared for all eventualities and try to prevent negative situations from arising in the first place.

Do not leave your dog alone outside to bark incessantly at the neighbours, for example. Instead, stay with him and give reassurance that all is well around the grounds. With your voice and body language, show the dog that there is nothing to fear when people walk past the gate. Your dog will take his cues from you, so set a good example. If

you want your dog to behave in a certain way, encourage the behaviour and lavish the dog with praise when he performs as you want.

If you want to eliminate undesirable behaviours, ignore them. Try not to reassure your dog too much if he displays nervous behaviour, as you may be inadvertently telling the dog that there is something to fear. Instead, ignore the dog until he is calm and then praise him.

Your adult dog will probably be house trained already, although this is not always the case. If the dog is not house trained, apply the same rules given above for training a puppy. For more information on training, see Chapter 6.

Do not allow your English Springer to free run until you are confident that he will come back to you.

of days, however, consult your vet.

Most Springer Spaniels have a very healthy appetite and immediately fall in love with the hand that feeds them, but there is the odd one that may need a little encouragement. Using boiled water for the first three days is a good idea for older dogs as well as for puppies. Keep a couple of tins of a bland dog food (possibly one that is fish-based) in the cupboard in case the dog suffers from loose bowel motions. Again, contact a vet should this continue.

EXERCISE

An English Springer can get a lot of exercise from running around at home, where he can run free in your well-fenced garden. However, there is no substitute for daily walks, and most English Springers live for their walks. Whatever the weather, daily exercise cannot be postponed. Even if you are unwell, your dog will expect and need a considerable amount of exercise. An English Springer will run all day if allowed, but a formal walk of about one hour will keep him in good shape. Try to include some roadwork in busy areas when walking your dog. This will give you opportunities for socialisation, where the dog can meet other dogs, people, bicycles, pushchairs, and traffic, etc.

Keep your dog on a lead for the first week or so, until you are confident that you have established a rapport. If the dog has a good recall, you can then let him off lead. If not, progress to a long line/extending lead until you have trained the recall and your dog is reliable. Most Springers are very willing to please, and you can use this to your advantage. Whenever your dog comes when called in your house and garden, reinforce the behaviour with dog treats. Then extend this to areas beyond the home.

LIVING WITH CHILDREN

Puppies seem to have a natural affinity with children, but your adult dog may not. Be prepared for the fact that your dog may not accept small children as readily as he does adults. Even if you have a dog that loves children and seems 'bomb-proof', make sure that he is never left alone with small children, and do not let children hold the dog's lead unless they are under very direct supervision.

Make sure that children understand that the dog must not be disturbed when he is in his bed or crate, and be extra vigilant when the dog is playing with a special toy. Most Springer Spaniels love children and enjoy playing with them, but an exuberant dog that has a habit of jumping up can easily knock over and frighten a child.

Right from the start, make sure that the dog knows and accepts that all humans, regardless of age, are higher in the pecking order that himself. You can reinforce this by involving the children in training exercises and getting them to give rewards to the dog when he performs a task successfully. Just as important is to teach the children to respect the dog. They must be made to realise that he is not a toy.

Hopefully, your adult dog will make the adjustment to his new life with ease, and you will enjoy your latest addition. However, remember that rescue centre staff are always on hand to answer any questions you may have and to help you overcome any problems that may arise. There will always be someone at the end of a telephone who can give you help and support.

It is a good idea to involve children with simple training exercises.

THE BEST OF CARE

5

Chapter

Having taken on the responsibility of dog ownership, it is essential for the owner to provide their dog with the very best of care. This includes feeding a nutritionally balanced diet, providing regular opportunities for exercise and mental stimulation, and grooming.

UNDERSTANDING NUTRITION

Correct nutrition for any breed of dog is very important. Indeed, if an average human baby grew at a rate comparable to some dog breeds, it has been estimated that the baby would be approaching 300kg by the time it is 18 months old. With this growth rate in mind, it is obvious why a good feeding and exercise regime are vital from the moment you bring your English Springer Spaniel home.

WHAT ARE NUTRIENTS?

A nutrient may be defined as a food constituent that helps to support life. They accomplish this by acting on structural components (muscle, bone, cells, etc), transporting substances throughout the body, regulating temperature, affecting palatability, and supplying energy. The nutrients your dog requires include:

- **Water:** This is the most important nutrient. Generally, a dog will require two to three parts of water for each part of dry food. The main function of water is to transport nutrients around the body and to excrete waste products.
- **Proteins:** These are essential for growth and repair of body tissue. They also provide energy.
- **Carbohydrates:** These are used for energy provision.
- **Fats and oils:** These supply energy in its most concentrated form. They also aid in the absorption of some vitamins.
- **Vitamins and minerals:** Due to the small quantities required, these are termed 'micronutrients'. They do not provide energy but they are essential for a wide range of physiological processes. For example, calcium and phosphorus are used in the make-up of teeth and bones.

Some nutrients can fulfil more than one function. For example, fats and carbohydrates both supply energy, but may also be used for storage. Water and some essential minerals are needed for all functions, except supplying energy.

Approximately 50-80 per cent of dry food intake is used for energy, and so the provision of the correct proportions of energy-yielding nutrients (protein,

Dogs require a combination of essential nutrients to stay fit and healthy.

carbohydrate and fat) is essential. Insoluble carbohydrates (e.g. fibre) do not provide energy, but they play an important part in the digestive system. They are used to prevent constipation – they attract water to the gut to ease the passing of bowel movements, although too much fibre may result in diarrhoea. Fibre also influences the movement of food through the gut. The type and quality of the fibre used affects the absorption of nutrients, with good-quality fibre providing optimal absorption.

Disadvantages of too much fibre in the diet include increased faecal weight, decreased energy density, decreased food transit time and decreased digestibility of protein, fat and soluble carbohydrate.

LIFE-STAGE FEEDING

As your English Springer puppy matures, his dietary requirement will change significantly. Small and often is the order of the day when it comes to feeding puppies, but it isn't just the frequency and size of meals that will alter as the dog grows older. The nutrient requirement of a puppy differs from that of an adult Springer with normal activity levels, and is different again for a working dog, pregnant or lactating bitch, or a Springer of advanced years.

To understand why this change is necessary, we can compare the English Springer to a human. Would a baby cope with one meal a day in the evening, even a sirloin beef dinner with all the trimmings? Similarly, how many

adults would cope with pureed vegetables, whether they were fed five times a day or not? It is easy to see why a dog should be treated like a human – that it has changing nutritional needs as it grows. The problem lies in distinguishing between when we should treat Springers like people, and when we should remember they are dogs.

PUPPIES

For the first three weeks of their life, puppies receive all the nourishment they require from their mother's milk. The 'first milk' or colostrum also contains maternal antibodies, which give essential early immunity to the puppies. The bitch's milk is very rich, and, in the event that she is unable to feed the puppies, a suitable bitch-milk replacement must be used. As with human babies, cow's milk is totally unsuitable for puppies.

At about three weeks of age the breeder will start to wean the puppies. Nowadays there are some excellent products on the market that aid this process. Puppy porridge or soaked and liquidised complete puppy foods are all suitable. However, some breeders add a little raw beef mince to whet the puppies' appetite. No matter what food the puppies are weaned on, for the first few days they will look quite unsightly directly after meal times – they seem to wear more than they have eaten.

The weaning food and the diet given during the early stages will have a relatively high-protein

SOURCES OF NUTRIENTS

To understand canine nutrition, it is important to take into account the dog's evolution. Dogs are descended from wolves, and even today there is a strong similarity between the lifestyle of the wolf and wild dogs. Most pet dogs are kept singly or in pairs and are fed with commercial dog food. Before domestication, however, the dog's ancestors would have lived in a pack, obtaining their food through hunting, although scavenging also provided some meals. Nearly all of the animal's carbohydrates would have been derived from semi-digested vegetation found in the gut of the prey. The flesh of the prey would have provided the required protein, fats and some of the vitamins and minerals, the remainder being derived from the bones.

CARBOHYDRATES
The best sources of soluble carbohydrates (starch) for the modern dog are corn, rice and wheat. Fibre or insoluble carbohydrate can be obtained from vegetable pulp, which provides a good fibre mixture. Some other fibre sources, such as peanut hulls or soya-based material, may act as irritants.

FATS
A good source of fats and oils comes from the fat of animal tissue, as this contains the essential fatty acids, linoleic acid and arachidonic acid. All animals require linoleic acid. It comprises 15-20 per cent of poultry and pork fat and it is also common in vegetable oil. Beef tallow is another good food from which to derive fat, although the quality may not be as good as other sources, and it may be deficient in one or more of the essential fatty acids.

PROTEIN
The quality of the protein in the diet is as important as the quantity. Good-quality protein is easily digested, has a high biological value, and contains a high proportion of essential amino acids. Foods containing high-quality protein include chicken, egg, chickenmeal and fish. Other sources of protein include cereal, soya and wheat, although the quality is not as high.

VITAMINS
Vitamins are found in differing quantities in various foods. No single food will supply them all. Commercially produced dog food contains them all, because it is a mixture of many different foods. Sources of vitamins include liver and egg for vitamins A, D and E; while meat, liver, eggs, fish, leafy vegetables, and cereals provide a good source of the B vitamins. There is no need to supply vitamin C in the diet, as dogs, in conjunction with most other animals, can make their own.

Feeding a diet rich in raw ingredients will provide a ready source of most of the minerals required, although beware of foods with a high ash content as this may lead to a lesser mineral quality.

Initially puppies get all the nourishment they need from their mother's milk.

content. This is to provide the essential amino acids the puppy requires for growth of muscle and bone, etc. Also present should be sufficient calcium, a mineral essential for the development of bone and teeth. At this point it is important to mention that calcium does not work alone in this function, so phosphorus and vitamin D must also be available in the correct proportions.

By the time the puppy leaves for his new home, he should be completely independent of his mother, nutritionally speaking. He is then ready to start a new life with a new family.

Your English Springer puppy should be fed a suitable puppy food until about six months of age, by which time he should have achieved most of his growing potential. It is important to remember that the puppy will require higher quantities of highly digestible, quality protein together with a high-quality fat content. These should be complemented by a balanced intake of calcium and phosphorus.

ADOLESCENTS

The next stage of growth and development is the adolescent or junior stage. Your English Springer should now have achieved his full height, so growth in an upward direction should have ceased. Your teenage Springer now needs only to fill-out and develop. As a result, the dog still needs a nutrient-rich diet, although it will be slightly lower in its content of vitamins and minerals. There should also be decreased levels of protein and fat.

ADULTS

As the mature, adult stage is reached, your English Springer requires a maintenance diet, one that will provide him with all the nutrients essential for everyday life, but will not result in excess weight gain. At this time, we must ensure we balance our Springer's requirements with the intake of nutrients – something over which the owner must take control, as your Springer will reach the conclusion that the intake is never enough!

VETERANS

As your Springer approaches his senior years, we must be aware that changes are taking place inside the dog – even though his attitude to life will belie his advancing years. There will be a lower energy requirement, due to decreased activity. It is important to take this consideration into account, so that your veteran Springer does not gain excess weight, which will put extra strain on his vital organs and ageing bones.

Many of the senior foods available provide a 'light' diet, in calorific terms, and also ensure that the food is highly palatable. The quality of the constituents is more important than the quantity, and a high-quality protein provision is especially critical as this will put less strain on the kidneys, a fact essential to the well-being of the ageing Springer.

COMMERCIAL LIFE-STAGE DIETS

Many popular pet food brands supply a full range of 'life-stage' foods, starting with a puppy food, following through the junior and maintenance formulas, and finishing with a senior diet.

Some manufacturers also offer diets for working or performance dogs and pregnant or lactating bitches. All are carefully developed and contain the right quantity and proportion of all the nutrients. It is important to realise that the addition of any supplements will unbalance any proprietary diet, and, far from being beneficial, will do your dog no favours at all.

TYPES OF DIET

How are you going to give your English Springer the nutrients he requires? What sort of dietary choices are there? Which is the best one for you to use? These are some of the points that the new owner will want to consider: will you use a complete diet? Do you think canned food and biscuit will be better? What about the much-publicised BARF ('biologically appropriate raw food', also known as 'bones and raw food') diet, and the benefits it will give to your puppy?

No matter what diet you decide to use, undoubtedly there will be a wealth of scientific evidence backing its suitability. Indeed, we must now question whether the move from feeding scraps to canned food and biscuit, then to muesli complete foods, extruded kibble, premium foods and almost complete circle to the BARF diet, is actually progression or just fashion.

An English Springer grows very rapidly during his first six months of life.

BREEDER'S CHOICE

After collecting your new puppy, you will arrive home full of information and good intentions. The breeder will have supplied you with an information sheet about diet and worming, and should have given you some food for the puppy so that his diet remains unchanged, especially for the first few days. It is not unusual for a puppy to have a little upset stomach for the first day or two in his new environment. It would be pure folly and asking for trouble to expect a puppy to cope with a diet change in the early days in his new home.

Complete food is formulated to suit dogs at different life stages.

A home-produced diet must contain all the essential nutrients your dog needs.

Biscuit and canned food must be fed in the correct ratio.

COMPLETE FOODS

Complete foods will provide your Springer with the correct balance of nutrients that he requires. They are convenient, readily available, and probably the most cost-effective way of feeding. They are available in muesli and extruded-kibble form, and come in an amazing array of colours. There is a great deal of variation in the cost of different brands, so how do you know which is best? There is no correct answer to this – each manufacturer will tell you that theirs is. Even the top breeders have different experiences of different foods, so

it is really a question of personal choice. When you analyse the composition of each product, it becomes apparent that, no matter the name on the bag, the majority of the complete foods available are owned by a small number of the largest companies in the foods and household goods sector!

Beware the quality of ingredients in the 'super-cheap' range. The nutrient content of the food, as stated on the packaging, must be accurate, to comply with food law. However, the quality of the nutrients does not have to be stated.

Manufacturers can obtain their ingredients from whichever supplier is cheaper on any given day. This means that the quality of a food can vary considerably over time. In the 'premium' range diets, the source of any particular ingredient is constant and guaranteed, and will not change in line with daily market trends.

CANNED MEAT AND BISCUIT

Feeding canned meat and biscuit meals is a tried-and-tested method of feeding dogs. Prior to the development of so many types of extruded complete food, it was probably the most popular

A BARF diet is based on a completely natural diet of raw meat and bones.

way to provide a dog with a balanced diet. One important difference between canned meat and biscuit and complete food is that you have to get the balance right and provide the correct proportions of biscuit and meat – otherwise you may have a weight problem on your hands.

HOME-PRODUCED

Home-produced diets – probably one of the earliest methods of feeding man's best friend, can also be a very effective way of feeding your Springer, if done correctly. There are, however, several potential pitfalls that must be avoided at all cost. A home-produced diet must be effective – in monetary terms, time and convenience – as well as being nutritionally balanced. It is worth remembering that commercial pet-food manufacturers have spent millions of pounds employing canine nutritionists to develop balanced diets of very high quality. Home-produced diets can be superb when the balance is right. That said, unless you are prepared to use a tried-and-tested recipe, you could be doing your much-loved dog no favours.

BARF

It has been suggested that a reversion to the BARF (biologically appropriate raw food) diet, almost taking the dog back to its wolf ancestry, will reduce the incidence of disease, enabling the dog to build up his own resistance. Many people now advocate feeding raw chicken wings as part of the daily ration. Although this raw meat will contain many of the required nutrients, you must be aware that there will be a complete lack of dietary fibre, and this is probably best given as pureed vegetable pulps.

MAKING THE CHOICE

For a healthy, adult dog, the choice of diet will be entirely the owner's, depending on their own personal preference. Does the ease of feeding, simplicity of storage, and provision of a readily available, balanced diet outweigh your perception that a dog should be fed as naturally as possible? Is the thought of providing your Springer with raw ingredients in a balanced form so appealing and important that you are able to justify the extra time for food preparation and the need for proper food storage facilities? This may be compounded by the fact that the cost of feeding one dog in this manner will far exceed the cost per dog if you were feeding a larger number the same way!

It has been discovered relatively recently that certain diseases alter a dog's nutritional requirements dramatically. The prevalence or incidence of one of these conditions may play an important part in the decision of how the dog is fed. Your vet will be able to advise you in this instance.

When your puppy first arrives home he will need four meals a day.

FEEDING REGIME

How many times a day does an English Springer need feeding? How much food should be given? The answers to these questions, of course, will depend on the age of the dog.

PUPPIES

For a fully weaned puppy up to the age of about 12 weeks, I would suggest four meals per day. When the puppies go to their new homes I suggest that the meals should be evenly spaced throughout the day, with the last meal not being immediately before bedtime (for toilet purposes). That said, I also advocate that it is very important for the puppy to fit in with the family routine – it is not necessary for the family to rearrange their life to accommodate the puppy.

The age at which the number of meals is reduced is also approximate, as some puppies will automatically eat less as they grow. From about 12 weeks of age, three meals per day should be sufficient, but you must remember to increase the size of the meals accordingly. It is at this stage, or shortly after, that a Springer puppy fed on one of the proprietary puppy complete meals can be introduced to the next life-stage diet – the junior diet. In doing so, you will be not only accommodating the slight change in nutritional requirements, you will also be introducing your puppy to a slightly larger kibble size, something the average Springer youngster (with the correspondingly voracious appetite) should treat as a welcome change.

ADOLESCENTS AND ADULTS

At about six months of age, your Springer puppy should be on two meals a day, and by now should definitely be on a junior diet. Some Springers may have reached their full height by this time, while others will have some way to go. Quantities required will be as individual as the dogs themselves. I am a firm believer that, at this age – and, indeed, any age up to about 12 months – dogs should be tending towards the plump, rather than the lean!

If you decide that you want your adult Springer to be fed once a day – morning or evening, depending on what fits in with your lifestyle – this is something that can be introduced at, or after, the dog's first birthday. Many breeders feed their adult dogs once a day, while others will keep their adults on two meals per day for the remainder of their lives. This is a decision that only you, as the owner, can make. Decide what is best for you and your Springer.

Ad-lib feeding – leaving down a bowl of food, albeit a rationed amount – is another method of feeding that suits some people. The theory is that the dog will eat only when he is hungry – and will choose to eat little and often. Theories are all very well, but they tend not to be appreciated by the average Springer! For very young puppies ad-lib feeding is not something I recommend, as it may lead to rather fussy puppies. As far as I am concerned, the only way to ensure good early development, is to let puppies get used to having a full belly.

If you feed your Springer a balanced diet and give regular exercise, you will be rewarded by owning a fit, active dog.

THE DANGERS OF OBESITY

One of the major pitfalls likely to be encountered by the new owner is not going to be *what*, but *how much*. It never ceases to amaze me how some people feel that, if a certain amount of anything is good, more will be better. It can be quite distressing for a breeder to see a puppy they have sold become not just a little on the plump side, as you advised, but rather more approaching the physically grotesque. On the other hand, much as we may be keen to encourage some weight loss (something much easier to accomplish in the younger dog than in the older dog), it is also possible for a new owner to feed too little in a bid to keep down a dog's weight. Moderation is the order of the day.

As previously stated, my personal preference is to see a chubby puppy, but an overweight adult is something I find quite unacceptable. There is nearly always a good reason for the dog's excess weight – lack of exercise is the most common. You must remember that your Springer's nutritional requirements will be, in the main, determined by his lifestyle. In other words, if there is a change in the daily activity levels for whatever reason, it is imperative that there is a corresponding reduction in the daily rations.

The problems caused by obesity are numerous, but a few of the more obvious ones are heart conditions, joint problems, diabetes and kidney problems. Although these conditions may occur in any dog, if you allow your Springer to become obese, you are undoubtedly increasing the possibility of their incidence.

GROOMING

Compared to many breeds of dog, the English Springer Spaniel is a relatively low-maintenance breed. That said, there is a certain amount of grooming that must be carried out to keep your Springer in tip-top condition.

COAT CARE

Coat care of the English Springer is not difficult, even for the novice pet owner. Indeed, if you feel overwhelmed by caring for your dog's coat, there are professional groomers who, for a nominal fee, will do it for you.

START YOUNG

Most dogs, if you start early enough, will enjoy their grooming sessions. I get quite annoyed when a dog of six or eight months is presented to me with the phrase, "He doesn't like being brushed, and won't allow us to do it!" The solution is to start as soon as you take the puppy home. Like socialisation in general, the more a puppy experiences in his early life, the more he will take things in his stride as an adult. Quality breeders normally start this process before the puppies leave to go to their new homes, so there is no excuse.

Whenever one of the puppies I have bred is leaving to go to his new home, I give a short demonstration. I place the pup on a table or worktop with a non-slip surface, steady the puppy under the chin, and gently rub my hands over his body as if I were grooming it. A soft bristle brush instead of the hand can follow this. A fine comb should be used to go through the ear and leg feathering. Due to the relative lack of coat present on your English Springer puppy, grooming at this age should be made into a fun activity, in order for him to become prepared for later.

The grooming equipment required to keep your English Springer Spaniel's coat in good condition can be kept to a minimum, but you should buy high-quality items, as, in addition to their suitability, these will be far more cost-effective in the long run. Please ensure, however, that you store them safely, as in typically Springer fashion, your much-loved pride and joy will take great delight in chewing – sometimes almost beyond recognition – any of the grooming equipment within his reach! You will probably find your new addition is quite selective, however, and will tend to favour the most expensive item.

EQUIPMENT

Essential items for your grooming kit would be a bristle brush, combs (normal and fine-toothed), a slicker brush and a pair of straight-edged scissors. Take care when purchasing the slicker – some of them are, in my opinion, far too hard. I usually suggest that if you feel uncomfortable when dragging the slicker firmly across your hand, so will your dog. With the straight-edged scissors, you may well be advised to purchase a pair with rounded ends for safety purposes – yours as well as the dog's.

GROOMING TIPS

Grooming is very important no matter what breed of dog you have. Even short-coated dogs benefit tremendously. The tools you use to achieve the best results will change depending on the coat type, but one of the most important effects of grooming is stimulation of the skin and hair follicles. This can be likened to a massage. Regular grooming will ensure that the natural oils of the dog's coat give your Springer a lovely sheen.

I use the slicker brush mainly for grooming through the feathering on the ears, the back of the front legs, under the body, and between the hind legs. With the brush in one hand, place your other hand the other side of

It is important to accustom your puppy to grooming from an early age.

the leg to support it. If you cannot feel the pins of the brush on your supporting hand, this should tell you that the brush hasn't gone right through the coat.

You will need to use the slicker on the body coat only on rare occasions. There is one very important fact to remember about Springers – they love to be disgusting. They eat disgusting things and can smell disgusting when they have rolled in something. Very few Springers can resist fox poo – the smellier it is, the more they roll in it, and

no matter how you pride yourself in your ability to train your Springer, even when called repeatedly he will seem to develop temporary deafness in the face of fox faeces. If you use the slicker brush on the body coat to remove something your dog has rolled in, do so with care. Scratching the skin will cause distress, and the last thing you want is to put your dog off grooming sessions.

Combs should be used for keeping the feathering completely knot free. I use it after I have used the slicker. Used properly,

ROUTINE GROOMING

A rake can be used to remove dead hair.

A slicker brush is ideal for working through feathering on the ears, legs, and under the body.

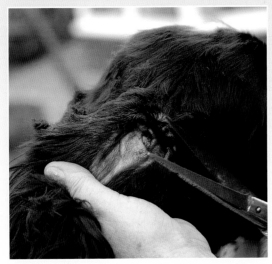

Hair that grows inside the ears should be trimmed to allow air to circulate.

Trim the hair that grows between on the underside of the feet so that it lies level with the pads.

the fine comb will remove any dead hairs present. When using the comb, keep it flat to the dog's body, placing a finger along the top of the comb, which will help remove dead hair. Never hold the comb perpendicularly to the skin, as this may scratch the dog.

Another good tool for removing dead hair from the body coat while massaging the skin is a rubber hound glove. These fit nicely over your hand and are covered with small rubber protrusions. The friction caused by the rubber on the dog's coat will loosen and remove dead hair, while the rubber bristles stimulate and massage the skin.

Areas of the coat requiring particular attention to ensure they do not become knotted are under the front legs, and right up behind the ears. On the subject of ears, please ensure that you remove any thick hair from inside the ears. The more air circulation your Springer gets in this area, the less chance there is of any ear problems.

Very often in liver-and-white or liver, white-and-tan Springers, the coat takes on a woolly appearance, especially in the summer months. This is due to bleaching by the sun. However, the fine comb, used as described earlier, will remove the majority of the dead hair to reveal the new healthy, shiny coat underneath.

The straight-edged

scissors can be used to remove the hair from the underside of the feet. The hair should be cut level with the pads. For the average Springer owner, this can save a great deal of work – it never ceases to amaze me just how much mud a Springer can carry into the house on his feet. The less hair protruding, the less chance your Springer's feet have of being dirt magnets.

BATHING

Never bath your Springer more than twice a year – this is the rule of thumb that those 'in the know' will tell you. The reason for this is that bathing removes essential oils from the coat. My advice to new owners is: if the

SHOW PRESENTATION

I f you are going to show your English Springer, you will need to work on his coat on a daily basis in order to achieve the smooth outlines that will enhance his appearance. Exhibitors build up grooming experience over many years, so if you want to take on the task of preparing your Springer for the show ring, you will need considerable dedication. The best course of action is to seek advice from your puppy's breeder who may be prepared to teach you. Beware of taking your dog to a professional groomer, unless the groomer has direct experience of preparing an English Springer Spaniel for the show ring.

dog needs a bath, give it one. Regular grooming will keep the coat relatively clean – but there's nothing like a good scrub to make them smell a lot fresher, especially if they have been rolling in something you'd prefer not to be reminded of every time they are within smelling distance.

The way you bath a Springer is, to my mind, far more important than the frequency of bathing.

When bathing my own dogs I use a medicated or insecticidal shampoo specifically for dogs. However, I make sure it is well diluted – most of the time far more dilute than the manufacturer's instructions. I also use special rubber brushes, which can be held in the palm of the hand and are available quite cheaply, to really scrub the dog. To bathe the dog effectively, it is better to use less soap and more 'elbow grease'. This has the added effect of really massaging the skin, which is as important as getting the hair clean.

After shampooing the dog, it is essential to rinse out the soap thoroughly. Every last trace of shampoo must be removed. One way to ensure that the coat is clean is to listen to it. Well-rinsed hair will 'squeak', which you can both hear and 'feel' when you run the hair between finger and thumb. This is where the expression 'squeaky clean' comes from.

SHOW PRESENTATION

It takes a lot of hard work to prepare an English Springer Spaniel for the show ring.

HANDSTRIPPING

Dead hair is plucked from the coat using finger and thumb.

The groomer must work through the whole coat, plucking out dead hair so that the coat lies close to the body.

CLIPPING

The English Springer should be clean throated, and this is best achieved using clippers.

THINNING

Thinning scissors are used to remove excess hair so that the head appears as a smooth contour.

Clippers can also be used to trim hair on the ears.

The hair behind the ears is thinned out so that the ears lie close to the side of the head.

SCISSORING

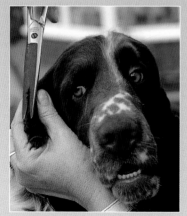

Straight-edged scissors are used to trim the edges of the ears.

If the tail is docked, it should be trimmed to give a smooth outline.

The feathering on the hind legs will need attention.

The feathering on the front legs needs to be tidied up, and hair on the undercarriage should also be trimmed.

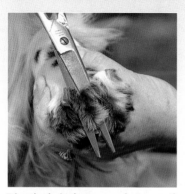

Trim the hair that grows between the toes to give feet a neat cat-like appearance.

The finished result: The English Springer should look neat and tidy, with smooth outlines, while still retaining a 'natural' look.

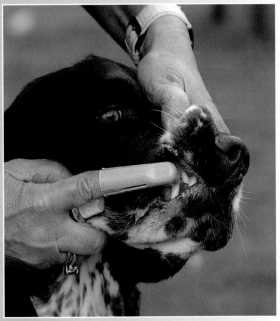

Check your Springer's teeth regularly, and clean them when necessary.

It is important to keep nails in trim.

A useful accessory for bathing your Springer is tomato ketchup. If your dog rolls in something disgusting – and believe me there's nothing worse than fox excrement – cover the offending area with tomato ketchup (before beginning bathing), leaving this to soak for a few minutes. After this time, shampoo and rinse as normal. By using the ketchup you will find that the smell disappears after one bath – otherwise three or four baths may be required.

TEETH

This is something that the average dog owner tends to overlook. Nonetheless, it should form part of the normal grooming routine. The condition of your Springer's teeth, and the frequency with which they will require cleaning, will be determined largely by the type of diet your dog eats. If you feed plenty of hard biscuit, or your dog eats bones, the teeth will be essentially self-cleaning. However, it is as well to check them regularly. Doggy toothpaste is nowadays readily available and there are even toothbrushes that fit over your finger like a thimble.

NAILS

Your Springer's nails may wear down naturally, but they should be checked each time you groom your dog. If they are overlong, they can cause discomfort. Your vet or groomer will be happy to clip the nails, but this is also something you can do yourself if you have trained your dog to accept having his feet handled. The two most popular types of nail clipper are the pliers-like type and the guillotine type, both of which are available from

A young puppy will run and play in short bursts, but he should not be subjected to lengthy exercise sessions.

pet shops. The main point to remember is not to cut too far back so that you cut into the nail bed or quick. If in doubt, remove tiny bits at a time. A styptic pencil (available from any chemist) is useful for stemming bleeding should you trim too much.

EXERCISE PLAN

In conjunction with the diet, exercise is a major factor in ensuring your new Springer puppy has a good start in life. In some ways, exercise may even be a more important consideration – I feel it falls into the 'if some is good then more is better' category.

Whenever someone buys one of my puppies, I advise that the puppy is not exercised too much for at least some of his formative months. If one examines a litter of wolf cubs, there is often a weaker or smaller one, but apart from the differences in the mature animals determined by sexual dimorphism (the male usually being larger than the female), the litter will all end up the same size and shape. If you look at a litter of Springer puppies, even those who are quite closely bred, they should,

in theory, be very similar; but by the time they have reached six to nine months, they are likely to be quite different in build and shape. What is the cause of this? Why the difference between wolves and dogs?

In a wolf litter, the cubs eat when their mother feeds them, but the rest of the time is essentially their own. They play when they want and they sleep when they want! For a puppy arriving in a new home, there is a certain amount of forced exercise. The moment you put your puppy on a lead, he will want to go for a walk – this is forced exercise. If

Allow your Springer to use his mind by combining physical exercise with mental stimulation.

you keep changing his routine, or you change the area where you exercise the puppy, he will want to explore everything. Again, this is forced exercise. Another major problem is that puppies pull when they are put on the lead for the first time. Prolonged periods of pulling will lead to development of the muscles around the shoulder far in advance of the muscular development in the hindquarters. This is one reason behind the number of young dogs of varying breeds who have a shape somewhat approaching a torpedo.

As I explained earlier in the chapter, puppies have different nutritional requirements to adults. At varying stages of your Springer's life these requirements alter further still. A puppy requires a high-quality diet to obtain the nutrients he needs for growth. Excess exercise results only in the puppy using the nutrients he needs for growth for energy release instead.

Personally speaking, I like to see young puppies running together freely – albeit for limited sessions. Little and often is the order of the day. This may not be possible once the puppy has left his littermates and gone to his new home, but a single puppy can get all the exercise he needs playing in an average-sized garden. Beyond this, I advocate that trips out and about should be done for reasons of socialisation, not exercise.

After about six months, your Springer can be walked regularly for further distances. Be sensible. How many people can walk a marathon without building up to the distance first? Start off with short walks and build them up gradually, over a period of several months. By the time your Springer is about 12 months old, he will be able to walk as far as you can.

English Springers were bred to retrieve from water, and they are excellent swimmers. Before allowing your Springer to swim, check the conditions are safe, and that there is an easy entrance and exit from the water.

PLAYTIME

I would suggest that play sessions are much more important than exercise for the young English Springer puppy. Play gives your dog the opportunity to exercise his brain as well as his body. If you have taken the time and trouble to obtain your puppy from a reputable breeder, your new addition should be relatively well adjusted by the time you get him home.

Do not be alarmed, however, if your puppy appears to be a little unsure when you first get him home – this is perfectly normal and will pass with time.

It is down to you to get your Springer accustomed to as many different situations as you can. Encourage him to play with toys. The array of different types, sizes and colours is now quite astonishing. Dumbbells are good, but take care – it doesn't take the average Springer very long to work out how to get the bell out. Swimming is another form of exercise that most Springers enjoy, especially if combined with retrieving from the water. 'Problem-solving' toys – such as balls that have to be rolled around the floor in order for bits of food to fall out – are another popular choice and can occupy your pet for some time.

SUMMARY

A good breeder will have put a great deal of consideration into providing Springer puppies that will give their new owners years of enjoyment with few problems. Good breeders will also give you sound advice on feeding, exercising, socialising and training. Please take this advice. The breeder has laid down the foundations, but the rest of the dog's health and happiness for the rest of his life is your responsibility.

A caring owner will build on the foundations laid down by the breeder.

TRAINING AND SOCIALISATION

Chapter 6

When you decided to bring an English Springer Spaniel into your life, you probably had dreams of how it was going to be: long walks together, cosy evenings with a Springer lying devotedly at your feet, and whenever you returned home, there would always be a special welcome waiting for you.

There is no doubt that you can achieve all this – and much more – with a Springer, but like anything that is worth having, you must be prepared to put in the work. A Springer Spaniel, regardless of whether it is a puppy or an adult, does not come ready trained, understanding exactly what you want and fitting perfectly into your lifestyle. A Springer has to learn his place in your family and he must discover what is acceptable behaviour.

We have a great starting point in that the Springer has an outstanding temperament. The breed was developed to be a biddable shooting companion, and all Springers share a friendly, eager-to-please nature. The Springer is also an intelligent dog, so we have all the ingredients needed to produce a well-trained, well-behaved companion.

THE FAMILY PACK

Dogs have been domesticated for some 14,000 years, but, luckily for us, they have inherited and retained behaviour from their distant ancestor – the wolf. A Springer Spaniel may never have lived in the wild, but he is born with the survival skills and the mentality of a meat-eating predator who hunts in a pack. A wolf living in a pack owes its existence to mutual co-operation and an acceptance of a hierarchy, as this ensures both food and

protection. A domesticated dog living in a family pack has exactly the same outlook. He wants food, companionship, and leadership – and it is your job to provide for these needs.

YOUR ROLE

Theories about dog behaviour and methods of training go in and out of fashion, but in reality, nothing has changed from the day when wolves ventured in from the wild to join the family circle. The wolf (and equally the dog) accepts a subservient place in the family pack in return for food and protection. In a dog's eyes, you are his leader, and he relies on you to make all the important decisions. This does not mean that you have to act like a dictator or a bully. You are accepted as a leader, without argument, as long as you have the right credentials.

The first part of the job is easy.

Can you be a firm, fair and consistent leader?

You are the provider, and you are therefore respected because you supply food. In a Springer's eyes, you must be the ultimate hunter because a day never goes by when you cannot find food. The second part of the leader's job description is straightforward, but for some reason we find it hard to achieve. In order for a dog to accept his place in the family pack he must respect his leader as the decision-maker. A low-ranking pack animal does not question authority; he is perfectly happy to see someone else shoulder the responsibility. Problems will only arise if you cut a poor figure as leader and the

dog feels he should mount a challenge for the top-ranking role.

HOW TO BE A GOOD LEADER

There are a number of guidelines to follow to establish yourself in the role of leader in a way that your Springer understands and respects. If you have a puppy, you may think you don't have to take this on board for a few months, but that would be a big mistake. Start as you mean to go on, and your pup will be quick to find his place in his new family.

- **Keep it simple:** Decide on the rules you want your Springer to obey and always make it

100 per cent clear what is acceptable, and what is unacceptable, behaviour.
- **Be consistent:** If you are not consistent about enforcing rules, how can you expect your Springer to take you seriously? There is nothing worse than allowing your Springer to jump up at you one moment and then scolding him the next time he does it because you are wearing your best clothes. As far as the Springer is concerned, he may as well try it on because he can't predict your reaction.
- **Get your timing right:** If you

are rewarding your Springer, and equally if you are reprimanding him, you must respond within one to two seconds otherwise the dog will not link his behaviour with your reaction (see page 95).

- **Read your dog's body language:** Find out how to read body language and facial expressions (see page 94) so that you understand your Springer's feelings and his intentions.

- **Be aware of your own body language:** You can help your dog to learn by using your body language to communicate with him. For example, if you want your dog to come to you, open your arms out and look inviting. If you want your dog to stay, use a hand signal (palm flat, facing the dog) so you are effectively 'blocking' his advance. Remember, the Springer is a highly intelligent dog, and has an uncanny knack of knowing your moods and your intentions before you have given out any obvious signals. For this reason, you must always try to keep one step ahead, and try to see the world from your dog's perspective.

- **Tone of voice:** Dogs are very receptive to tone of voice, so you can use your voice to praise him or to correct undesirable behaviour. If you are pleased with your Springer, praise him to the skies in a warm, happy voice. If you want to stop him raiding the

Ask your Springer to 'Wait' at doorways, so that he does not assert his authority by barging ahead.

bin, use a deep, stern voice when you say "No".

- **Give one command only:** If you keep repeating a command, or keeping changing it, your Springer will think you are babbling and will probably ignore you. If your Springer does not respond the first time you ask, make it simple by using a treat to lure him into position, and then you can reward him for a correct response.

- **Daily reminders:** A young, excitable Springer is apt to forget his manners from time to time, and an adolescent dog may attempt to challenge your authority (see page 106). Rather than coming down on your Springer like a ton of bricks when he does something wrong, try to prevent bad manners by daily reminders of good manners. For example:

i Do not let your dog barge ahead of you when you are going through a door.

ii Do not let him leap out of the car the moment you open the door (which could be potentially lethal, as well as being disrespectful).

iii Do not let him eat from your hand when you are at the table.

iv Do not let him 'win' a toy at the end of a play session and then make off with it. You 'own' his toys, and you must end every play session on your terms. If your Springer takes possession of a toy, do not confront him, demanding that he gives up the toy. This may fuel his determination to keep it. The best plan is to trade with him, substituting something equally desirable – a tasty piece of cheese or sausage – so that your Springer is happy to give up his toy. In this way, you have won the battle without the need for conflict.

UNDERSTANDING YOUR SPRINGER

Body language is an important means of communication between dogs, which they use to make friends, to assert status, and to avoid conflict. It is important to get on your dog's wavelength by understanding his body language and reading his facial expressions.

- A positive body posture and a wagging tail indicate a happy, confident dog.
- A crouched body posture with ears back and tail down show that a dog is being submissive. A dog may do this when he is being told off or if a more assertive dog approaches him.
- A bold dog will stand tall, looking strong and alert. His ears will be forward and his tail will be held high.
- A dog who raises his hackles (lifting the fur along his topline) is trying to look as scary as possible. This may be the prelude to aggressive behaviour, but, in many cases, the dog is apprehensive and is unsure how to cope with a situation.
- A playful dog will go down on his front legs while standing on his hind legs in a bow position. This friendly invitation says: "I'm no threat, let's play."
- A dominant, aggressive dog will meet other dogs with a hard stare. If he is challenged, he may bare his teeth and growl, and the corners of his mouth will be drawn forward. His ears will be forward and he will appear tense in every muscle (see page 112).
- A nervous dog will often show aggressive behaviour as a means of self-protection. If threatened, this dog will lower his head and flatten his ears. The corners of his mouth may be drawn back, and he may bark or whine.
- Some Springers are 'smilers', curling up their top lip and showing their teeth when they greet people. This should never be confused with a snarl, which would be accompanied by the upright posture of a dominant dog. A smiling dog will have a low body posture and a wagging tail; he is being submissive and it is a greeting that is often used when low-ranking animals greet high-ranking animals in a pack.

If you watch dogs interacting, you will start to understand canine body language.

GIVING REWARDS

Why should your Springer do as you ask? If you follow the guidelines given above, your Springer should respect your authority, but what about the time when he is playing with a new doggy friend or has found a really enticing scent? The answer is that you must always be the most interesting, the most attractive, and the most irresistible person in your Springer's eyes. It would be nice to think you could achieve this by personality alone, but most of us need a little extra help. You need to find out what is the biggest reward for your dog – in a Springer's case, it will nearly always be food – and to give him a treat when he does as you ask. For some dogs, the reward might be a play with a favourite toy, but, whatever it is, it must be something that your dog really wants.

When you are teaching a dog a new exercise, you should reward him frequently. When he knows the exercise or command, reward him randomly so that he keeps on responding to you in a positive manner. If your dog does something extra special, like leaving his canine chum mid-play in the park, make sure he really knows how pleased you are by giving him a handful of treats or throwing his ball a few extra times. If he gets a bonanza reward, he is more likely to come back on future occasions, because you have proved to be even more rewarding than his previous activity.

When you are training, you need to 'think dog' so that you motivate and reward your Springer.

TOP TREATS

Some trainers grade treats depending on what they are asking the dog to do. A dog may get a low-grade treat, such as a piece of dry food, to reward good behaviour on a random basis, such as sitting when you open a door or allowing you to examine his teeth. But high-grade treats, which may be cooked liver, sausage or cheese, are reserved for training new exercises or for use in the park when you want a really good recall. Whatever type of treat you use, remember to subtract it from your Springer's daily ration. Fat Springers are lethargic, prone to health problems, and will almost certainly have a shorter life expectancy. Reward your Springer, but always keep a check on his figure!

HOW DO DOGS LEARN?

It is not difficult to get inside your Springer's head and understand how he learns, as it is not dissimilar to the way we learn. Dogs learn by conditioning: they find out that specific behaviours produce specific consequences. This is known as operant conditioning or consequence learning. Consequences have to be immediate or clearly linked to the behaviour, as a dog sees the world in terms of action and result. Dogs will quickly learn if an action has a bad consequence or a good consequence.

Dogs also learn by association. This is known as classical conditioning or association learning. It is the type of learning made famous by Pavlov's experiment with dogs. Pavlov presented dogs with food and measured their salivary response (how much they drooled). Then he rang a bell just before presenting the food. At first, the dogs did not salivate until the food was presented. But after a while they learnt that the sound of the bell meant that food was coming, and so they salivated when they heard the bell. A dog needs to learn the association in order for it to have any meaning. For example, a dog that has never seen a lead before will be completely indifferent to it. A dog that has learnt that a lead means he is going for a walk will get excited the second he sees the lead; he has learnt to associate a lead with a walk.

BE POSITIVE

The most effective method of training dogs is to use their ability to learn by consequence and to teach that the behaviour you want produces a good consequence. For example, if you ask your Springer to "Sit", and reward him with a treat, he will learn that it is worth his while to sit on command because it will lead to a treat. He is far more likely to repeat the behaviour, and the behaviour will become stronger, because it results in a positive outcome. This method of training is known as positive reinforcement, and it generally

THE CLICKER REVOLUTION

Karen Pryor pioneered the technique of clicker training when she was working with dolphins. It is very much a continuation of Pavlov's work and makes full use of association learning.

Karen wanted to mark 'correct' behaviour at the precise moment it happened. She found it was impossible to toss a fish to a dolphin when it was in mid-air, when she wanted to reward it. Her aim was to establish a conditioned response so the dolphin knew that it had performed correctly and a reward would follow.

The solution was the clicker: a small matchbox-shaped training aid, with a metal tongue that makes a click when it is pressed. To begin with, the dolphin had to learn that a click meant that food was coming. The dolphin then learnt that it

must 'earn' a click in order to get a reward. Clicker training has been used with many different animals, most particularly with dogs, and it has proved hugely successful. It is a great aid for pet owners and is also widely used by professional trainers who teach highly specialised skills.

leads to a happy, co-operative dog that is willing to work, and a handler who has fun training their dog.

The opposite approach is negative reinforcement. This is far less effective and often results in a poor relationship between dog and owner. In this method of training, you ask your Springer to "Sit", and, if he does not respond, you deliver a sharp yank on the training collar or push his rear to the ground. The dog learns that not responding to your command has a bad consequence, and he may be less likely to ignore you in the future. However, it may well have a bad consequence for you, too. A dog that is treated in this way may associate harsh handling with the handler and become aggressive or fearful. Instead of establishing a pattern of willing co-operation, you are establishing a relationship built on coercion.

Try to find a training area that is free from distractions.

GETTING STARTED

As you train your Springer, you will develop your own techniques as you get to know what motivates him. You may decide to get involved with clicker training or you may prefer to go for a simple command-and-reward formula. It does not matter what form of training you use, as long as it is based on positive, reward-based methods.

There are a few important guidelines to bear in mind when you are training your Springer:

• Find a training area that is free from distractions, particularly

when you are just starting out.
• Keep training sessions short, especially with young puppies that have very short attention spans.
• Do not train if you are in a bad mood or if you are on a tight schedule – the training session will be doomed to failure. The Springer has a stubborn streak, and you need to keep the mood relaxed and happy to get the best results.
• If you are using a toy as a reward, make sure it is only available when you are

training. In this way it has an added value for your Springer.
• If you are using food treats, which is the best training aid for most Springer Spaniels, make sure they are bite-size and easy to swallow; you don't want to hang about while your Springer chews on his treat.
• All food treats must be deducted from your Springer's daily food ration.
• When you are training your English Springer, move around your allocated area so that your dog does not think that an

exercise can only be performed in one place.

- If your Springer is finding an exercise difficult, try not to get frustrated. Go back a step and praise him for his effort. You will probably find he is more successful when you try again at the next training session. Many owners say training a Springer is a case of taking one step forward, and two steps back, so you will need to be patient.
- Always end training sessions on a happy, positive note. Ask your Springer to do something you know he can do – it could be a trick he enjoys performing – and then reward him with a few treats or an extra-long play session.

In the exercises that follow, clicker training is introduced and followed, but all the exercises will work without the use of a clicker.

INTRODUCING A CLICKER

This is dead easy and the Springer, who loves his food, will learn about the clicker in record time! It can be combined with attention training, which is a very useful tool and can be used on many different occasions.

- Prepare some treats and go to an area that is free from distractions. When your Springer stops sniffing around and looks at you, click and reward by throwing him a treat. This means he will not crowd you, but will go looking for the treat. Repeat a few times. If your Springer is easily distracted, you may need to start this exercise with the dog on a lead.
- After a few clicks, your Springer understands that if he hears a click, he will get a treat. He must now learn that he must 'earn' a click. This time, when your Springer looks at you, wait a little longer before clicking, and then reward him. If your dog is on a lead but responding well, try him off the lead.
- When your Springer is working for a click and giving you his attention, you can introduce a cue or command word, such as "Watch". Repeat a few times, using the cue. You now have a Springer that understands the clicker and will give you his attention when you ask him to "Watch".

The first step in clicker training is to get your dog's attention.

Hold a treat above your Springer's head to lure him into the Sit.

Lower a treat to the ground, and your Springer should follow it, going into the Down.

TRAINING EXERCISES

THE SIT

This is the easiest exercise to teach, so it is rewarding for both you and your Springer.

- Choose a tasty treat and hold it just above your puppy's nose. As he looks up at the treat, he will naturally go into the Sit. As soon as he is in position, reward him.
- Repeat the exercise, and when your pup understands what you want, introduce the "Sit" command.
- You can practise at mealtimes by holding out the bowl and waiting for your dog to sit.

Most Springers learn this one very quickly!

THE DOWN

Work hard at this exercise because a reliable Down is useful in many different situations, and an instant Down can be a lifesaver.

- You can start with your dog in a Sit, or it is just as effective to teach it when the dog is standing. Hold a treat just below your puppy's nose, and slowly lower it towards the ground. The treat acts as a lure, and your puppy will follow it, first going down on his forequarters, and then bringing his hindquarters down

as he tries to get the treat.
- Make sure you close your fist around the treat, and only reward your puppy with the treat when he is in the correct position. If your puppy is reluctant to go Down, you can apply gentle pressure on his shoulders to encourage him to go into the correct position.
- When your puppy is following the treat and going into position, introduce a verbal command.
- Build up this exercise over a period of time, each time waiting a little longer before giving the reward, so the puppy learns to stay in the Down position.

THE RECALL

It is never too soon to start training the Recall. In fact, if you have a puppy it is best to start almost from the moment the puppy arrives home, as he has a strong instinct to follow you. Make sure you are always happy and excited when your Springer comes to you, even if he has been slower than you would like. Your Springer must believe that the greatest reward is coming to you.

- You can start teaching the Recall from the moment your puppy arrives home. He will naturally follow you, so keep calling his name and rewarding him when he comes to you.
- Practise in the garden, and when your puppy is busy exploring, get his attention by calling his name. As he runs towards you, introduce the verbal command "Come". Make sure you sound happy and exciting, so your puppy wants to come to you. When he responds, give him lots of praise.
- If your puppy is slow to respond, try running away a few paces, or jumping up and down. It doesn't matter how silly you look, the key issue is to get your puppy's attention, and then make yourself irresistible!
- In a dog's mind, coming when called should be regarded as the best fun because he

The aim is to train for an enthusiastic response to the Recall with your Springer bounding towards you.

SECRET WEAPON

You can build up a strong Recall by using another form of association learning. Buy a whistle, and when you are giving your English Springer his food, peep on the whistle. You can choose the type of signal you want to give: two short peeps or one long whistle, for example. Within a matter of days, your dog will learn that the sound of the whistle means that food is coming.

Now transfer the lesson outside. Arm yourself with some tasty treats and the whistle. Allow your Springer to run free in the garden, and, after a couple of minutes, use the whistle. The dog has already learnt to associate the whistle with food, so

he will come towards you. Immediately reward him with a treat and lots of praise. Repeat the lesson a few times in the garden so you are confident that your dog is responding before trying it in the park. Make sure you always have some treats in your pocket when you go for a walk, and your dog will quickly learn how rewarding it is to come to you.

knows he is always going to be rewarded. Never make the mistake of telling your dog off, no matter how slow he is to respond, as you will undo all your previous hard work.

- When you are free running your dog, make sure you have his favourite toy or a pocket full of treats, so you can reward him at intervals throughout the walk when you call him to you. Do not allow your dog to free run and only call him back at the end of the walk to clip his lead on. An intelligent Springer will soon realise that the Recall means the end of his walk, and then end of fun – so who can blame him for not wanting to come back?

TRAINING LINE

This is the equivalent of a very long lead, which you can buy at a pet store, or you can make your own with a length of rope. The training line is attached to your Springer's collar and should be around 15 feet (4.5 metres) in length.

The purpose of the training line is to prevent your Springer from disobeying you so that he never has the chance to get into bad habits. For example, when you call your Springer and he ignores you, you can immediately pick up the end of the training line and call him again. By picking up the line you will have attracted his attention, and if you call in an excited, happy voice, your Springer will come to you. The

moment he comes to you, give him a tasty treat so he is instantly rewarded for making the 'right' decision.

The training line is very useful when your Springer becomes an adolescent and is testing your leadership. When you have reinforced the correct behaviour a number of times, your dog will build up a strong recall and you will not need to use a training line.

WALKING ON A LOOSE LEAD

This is a simple exercise, which baffles many Springer owners. In most cases, owners are too impatient, wanting to get on with the expedition rather that training the dog how to walk on a lead. Take time with this one; a

With practice, your Springer will learn to walk on a loose lead, paying attention to you.

Springer that pulls on the lead is no pleasure to own.

- In the early stages of lead training, allow your puppy to pick his route and follow him. He will get used to the feeling of being 'attached' to you, and has no reason to put up any resistance.
- Next, find a toy or a tasty treat and show it to your puppy. Let him follow the treat/toy for a few paces, and then reward him.
- Build up the amount of time your pup will walk with you, and when he is walking nicely by your side, introduce the verbal command "Heel" or "Close". Give lots of praise when your pup is in the correct position.
- When your pup is walking alongside you, keep focusing his attention on you by using his name, and then rewarding him when he looks at you. If it is going well, introduce some changes of direction.
- Do not attempt to take your puppy out on the lead, until you have mastered the basics at home. You need to be confident that your puppy accepts the lead, and will focus his attention on you, when requested, before you face the challenge of a busy environment.
- As your Springer gets bigger and stronger, he may try to

pull on the lead, particularly if you are heading somewhere he wants to go, such as the park. If this happens, stop, call your dog to you, and do not set off again until he is in the correct position. It may take time, but your Springer will eventually realise that it is more productive to walk by your side, than to pull ahead.

STAYS

This may not be the most exciting exercise, but it is one of the most useful. There are many occasions when you want your Springer to stay in position, even if it is only for a few seconds. The classic example is when you want your Springer to stay in the back of the car until you have clipped his lead on. Some trainers use the verbal command "Stay" when the dog is to stay in position for an extended period of time, and "Wait" if the dog is to stay in position for a few seconds until you give the next command. Others trainers use a universal "Stay" to cover all situations. It all comes down to personal preference, and as long as you are consistent, your dog will understand the command he is given.

- Put your puppy in a Sit or a Down, and use a hand signal (flat palm, facing the dog) to show he is to stay in position. Step a pace away from the dog. Wait a second, step back and reward him. If you have a lively pup, you may find it easier to train this exercise on the lead.

- Repeat the exercise, gradually increasing the distance you can leave your dog. When you return to your dog's side, praise him quietly, and release him with a command, such as "OK".
- Remember to keep you body language very still when you are training this exercise, and avoid eye contact with your dog. Work on this exercise over a period of time, and you will build up a really reliable Stay.

Build up the Stay exercise in easy stages.

SOCIALISATION

While your Springer is mastering basic obedience exercises, there is other, equally important, work to do with him. A Springer is not only becoming a part of your home and family, he is becoming a member of the community. He needs to be able to live in the outside world, coping calmly with every new situation that comes his way. It is your job to introduce him to as many different experiences as possible, and encourage him to behave in an appropriate manner.

In order to socialise your Springer effectively, it is helpful to understand how his brain is developing, and then you will get a perspective on how he sees the world.

CANINE SOCIALISATION (Birth to 7 weeks)

This is the time when a dog learns how to be a dog. By interacting with his mother and his littermates, a young pup learns about leadership and submission. He learns to read body posture so that he understands the intentions of his mother and his siblings. A puppy that is taken away from his litter too early may always have behavioural problems with other dogs, either being fearful or aggressive.

SOCIALISATION PERIOD (7 to 12 weeks)

This is the time to get cracking and introduce your Springer puppy to as many different experiences as possible. This includes meeting different people, other dogs and animals, seeing new sights, and hearing a range of sounds, from the vacuum cleaner to the roar of traffic. At this stage, a puppy learns very quickly and what he learns will stay with him for the rest of his life. This is the best time for a puppy to move to a new home, as he is adaptable and ready to form deep bonds.

FEAR-IMPRINT PERIOD (8 to 11 weeks)

This occurs during the socialisation period, and it can be the cause of problems if it is not handled carefully. If a

Springer puppy is exposed to a frightening or painful experience, it will lead to lasting impressions. Obviously, you will attempt to avoid frightening situations, such as your pup being bullied by a mean-spirited older dog, or a firework going off, but you cannot always protect your puppy from the unexpected. If your pup has a nasty experience, the best plan is to make light of it and distract him by offering him a treat or a game. The pup will take the lead from you and will be reassured that there is nothing to worry about. If you mollycoddle him and sympathise with him, he is far more likely to retain the memory of his fear.

As soon as your puppy has completed his vaccinations, take him out and about so that he can learn about the world he is to live in.

SENIORITY PERIOD (12 to 16 weeks)

During this period, your Springer puppy starts to cut the apron strings and becomes more independent. He will test out his status to find out who is the pack leader: him or you. Bad habits, such as play biting, which may have been seen as endearing a few weeks earlier, should be firmly discouraged. Remember to use positive, reward-based training, but make sure your puppy knows that you are the leader and must be respected.

SECOND FEAR-IMPRINT PERIOD (6 to 14 months)

This period is not as critical as the first fear-imprint period, but it should still be handled carefully. During this time your Springer may appear apprehensive, or he may show fear of something familiar. You may feel as if you have taken a backwards step, but if you adopt a calm, positive manner, your Springer will see that there is nothing to be frightened of. Do not make your dog confront the thing that frightens him. Simply distract his attention, and give him something else to think about, such as obeying a simple command, such as "Sit" or "Down". This will give you the opportunity to praise and reward your dog, and will help to boost his confidence.

YOUNG ADULTHOOD AND MATURITY (1 to 4 years)

The timing of this phase depends on the size of the dog: the bigger

A well-socialised Springer will be calm and confident in all situations, and will love being part of family expeditions.

the dog, the later it is. This period coincides with a dog's increased size and strength, mental as well as physical. Some dogs, particularly those with a dominant nature, will test your leadership again and may become aggressive towards other dogs. Firmness and continued training are essential at this time so that your Springer accepts his status in the family pack.

IDEAS FOR SOCIALISATION

When you are socialising your Springer, you want him to experience as many different situations as possible. Try out some of the following ideas, which will ensure your Springer has an all-round education.

If you are taking on a rescued dog and have little knowledge of his background, it is important to work through a programme of socialisation. A young puppy soaks up new experiences like a sponge, but an older dog can still learn. If a rescued dog shows fear or apprehension, treat him in exactly the same way as you would treat a youngster who is going through the second fear-imprint period (see page 104).

- Accustom your puppy to household noises, such as the vacuum cleaner, the television and the washing machine.
- Ask visitors to come to the door, wearing different types of clothing – for example, wearing a hat, a long raincoat, or carrying a stick or an umbrella.
- If you do not have children at home, make sure your Springer has a chance to meet

and play with them. Go to a local park and watch children in the play area. You will not be able to take your Springer inside the play area, but he will see children playing and will get used to their shouts of excitement.
- Attend puppy classes. These are designed for puppies between the ages of 12 to 20 weeks, and give puppies a chance to play and interact together in a controlled, supervised environment. Your vet will have details of a local class.
- Take a walk around some quiet streets, such as a residential area, so your Springer can get used to the sound of traffic. As he becomes more confident, progress to busier areas.

TRAINING CLUBS

There are lots of training clubs to choose from. Your vet will probably have details of clubs in your area, or you can ask friends who have dogs if they attend a club. Alternatively, use the internet to find out more information. But how do you know if the club is any good?

Before you take your dog, ask if you can go to a class as an observer and find out the following:
- What experience does the instructor(s) have?
- Do they have experience with Springer Spaniels?
- Is the class well organised, and are the dogs reasonably quiet? (A noisy class indicates an unruly atmosphere, which will not be conducive to learning).
- Are there are a number of classes to suit dogs of different ages and abilities?
- Are positive, reward-based training methods used?
- Does the club train for the Good Citizen Scheme (see page 113).

If you are not happy with the training club, find another one. An inexperienced instructor who cannot handle a number of dogs in a confined environment can do more harm than good.

- Go to a railway station. You don't have to get on a train if you don't need to, but your Springer will have the chance to experience trains, people wheeling luggage, loudspeaker announcements, and going up and down stairs and over railway bridges.
- If you live in the town, plan a trip to the country. You can enjoy a day out and provide an opportunity for your Springer to see livestock, such as sheep, cattle and horses.
- One of the best places for socialising a dog is at a country fair. There will be crowds of people, livestock in pens, tractors, bouncy castles, fairground rides and food stalls.

- When your dog is over 20 weeks of age, find a training class for adult dogs. You may find that your local training class has both puppy and adult classes.

THE ADOLESCENT SPRINGER

It happens to every dog – and every owner. One minute you have an obedient well-behaved youngster, and the next you have a boisterous adolescent who appears to have forgotten everything he learnt. This applies equally to males and females, although the type of adolescent behaviour, and its onset, varies between individuals.

In most cases a Springer will hit adolescence at around six to eight months, and you can expect behavioural changes for at least a couple of months. With luck, your Springer will grow up and show signs of becoming a mature adult dog by 12 to 14 months. In reality, adolescence is not the nightmare period you may imagine, if you see it from your Springer's perspective.

Just like a teenager, an adolescent Springer feels the need to flex his muscles and challenge the status quo. He may become disobedient and break house rules as he tests your authority and your role as leader. Your response must be firm, fair and consistent. If you show that you are a strong leader (see page 91) and are quick to reward good behaviour, your Springer will accept you as his

protector and provider.
Remember, boredom is the
enemy, and if your Springer lacks
mental stimulation, his behaviour
will deteriorate as he finds ways to
amuse himself. It is your job to
provide sufficient exericise and
training to keep a young,
intelligent dog well occupied.

WHEN THINGS GO WRONG

Positive, reward-based training
has proved to be the most
effective method of teaching
dogs, but what happens when
your Springer does something
wrong and you need to show
him that his behaviour is
unacceptable? The old-fashioned
school of dog training used to
rely on the powers of
punishment and negative
reinforcement. A dog who raided
the bin, for example, was
smacked. Now we have learnt
that it is not only unpleasant
and cruel to hit a dog, it is also
ineffective. If you hit a dog for
stealing, he is more than likely
to see *you* as the bad
consequence of stealing, so he
may raid the bin again, but
probably not when you are
around. If he raided the bin
some time before you discovered
it, he will be even more
confused by your punishment,
as he will not relate your
response to his 'crime'.

A more commonplace example
is when a dog fails to respond to
a recall in the park. When the
dog eventually comes back, the
owner puts the dogs on the lead
and goes straight home to punish

A young Springer may be inclined to flex his muscles and test the boundaries.

the dog for his poor response.
Unfortunately, the dog will have a
different interpretation. He does
not think: "I won't ignore a recall
command because the bad
consequence is the end of my
play in the park." He thinks:
"Coming to my owner resulted in
the end of playtime – therefore
coming to my owner has a bad
consequence so I won't do that
again."

There are a number of
strategies to tackle undesirable
behaviour – and they have
nothing to do with harsh
handling.

Ignoring bad behaviour: A lot of
undesirable behaviour in young
Springers is learnt from their
owners. It is so easy to hype up
an excitable youngster, and most
owners don't even know they are

Despite all your care, there may be times when things go wrong and your Springer exhibits undesirable behaviour.

doing it. For example, visitors come to the door, and you make a great fuss, calling the dog, restraining him, telling him off for barking or jumping up. Before you know it, your Springer has learnt that the arrival of visitors is the signal for anarchy; he will match your mood, becoming more and more hyped up, and you have lost your position of authority. If your Springer becomes demanding and attention seeking, the best plan is to take all the tension out of the situation and ignore him. Do not look at him, do not speak to him, and do not push him down – all

these actions are rewarding for your Springer. But someone who turns their back on him and offers no response is plain boring. The moment your Springer stops barking, and has four feet on the ground, give him lots of praise and maybe a treat. If you repeat this often enough, the Springer will learn that jumping up and barking does not have any good consequences, such as getting attention. Instead he is ignored. However, when he is quiet and has all four feet on the ground, he gets loads of attention. He links the action with the consequence, and chooses the

action that is most rewarding. You will find that this strategy works well with all attention-seeking behaviour, such as whining or scrabbling at doors. Being ignored is a worst-case scenario for a Springer, so remember to use it as an effective training tool.

Stopping bad behaviour: There are occasions when you want to call an instant halt to whatever it is your Springer is doing. You may have caught him red-handed stealing food from the kitchen counter – although you will have to be quick as Springers are highly accomplished thieves. But in this instance, your dog has already committed the 'crime', so your aim is to stop him and to redirect his attention. You can do this by using a deep, firm tone of voice to say "No", which will startle him, and then call him to you in a bright, happy voice. If necessary, you can attract him with a toy or a treat. The moment your Springer stops the undesirable behaviour and comes towards you, you can reward his good behaviour. You can back this up by running through a couple of simple exercises, such as a Sit or a Down, and rewarding with treats. In this way, your Springer focuses his attention on you, and sees you as the greatest source of reward and pleasure.

In a more extreme situation, when you want to interrupt undesirable behaviour, and you know that a simple "No" will not do the trick, you can try something a little more dramatic. If you get a can and fill it with pebbles, it will make a really loud noise when you shake it or throw it. The same effect can be achieved with purpose-made training discs. The dog will be startled and stop what he is doing. Even better, the dog will not associate the unpleasant noise with you. This gives you the perfect opportunity to be the nice guy, calling the dog to you and giving him lots of praise.

PROBLEM BEHAVIOUR

If you have trained your Springer from puppyhood, survived his adolescence and established yourself as a fair and consistent leader, you will end up with a brilliant companion dog. The Springer is a well-balanced, out-going dog who is eager to please; he thrives on company, both human and canine, and likes nothing better than spending time with his owners.

However, problems may arise unexpectedly, or you may have taken on a rescued Springer that has established behavioural problems. If you are worried about your Springer and feel out of your depth, do not delay in seeking professional help. This is readily available, usually through a referral from your vet, or you can find out additional information on the internet (see Appendices for web addresses). An animal behaviourist will have experience in tackling problem behaviour and will be able to help both you and your dog.

SEPARATION ANXIETY

The Springer Spaniel loves his family, and so it is important that he learns to accept short periods of separation without becoming anxious. A new puppy should be left for short periods on his own, ideally in a crate where he cannot get up to any mischief. It is a good idea to leave him with a boredom-busting toy (see page 59) so he will be happily occupied in your absence. When you return, do not rush to the crate and make a huge fuss. Wait a few minutes, and then calmly go to the crate and release your dog, telling him how good he has been. If this scenario is repeated a number of times, your Springer will soon learn that being left on his own is no big deal. As your Springer grows up, keep to the routine of making minimum fuss when you leave the house, and ignoring your Springer for a few minutes when you return. In this way, your Springer learns to accept comings and goings as a matter of course.

Problems with separation anxiety are most likely to arise if you take on a rescued dog who has major insecurities. You may also find your Springer hates being left if you have failed to accustom him to short periods of isolation when he was growing up. Separation anxiety is expressed in a number of ways, and all are equally distressing for both dog and owner. An anxious dog who is left alone may bark and whine continuously, urinate and defecate, and may be extremely destructive.

ASSERTIVE BEHAVIOUR

If you have trained and socialised your Springer correctly, he will know his place in the family pack and will have no desire to

A boredom buster will help to keep your Springer occupied while you are away.

PROBLEM-SOLVING GUIDE

There are a number of steps you can take when attempting to help a dog overcome separation anxiety.

• Put up a baby-gate between adjoining rooms, and leave your dog in one room while you are

Use a stair-gate to accustom your Springer to short periods of separation when you are still in sight.

in the other room. Your dog will be able to see you and hear you, but he is learning to cope without being right next to you. Build up the amount of time you can leave your dog in easy stages.

• Buy some boredom-busting toys and fill them with some tasty treats. Whenever you leave your dog, give him a food-filled toy so that he is busy while you are away.

• If you have not used a crate before, it is not too late to start. Make sure the crate is big and comfortable, and train your Springer to get used to going in his crate while you are in the same room. Gradually build up the amount of time he spends in the crate, and then start leaving the room for short periods. When you return, do not make a fuss of your dog. Leave him for five or 10 minutes before releasing him so that he gets used to your comings and goings.

• Pretend to go out, putting on your coat and jangling keys, but do not leave the house. An anxious dog often becomes hyped up by the ritual of leave taking, and so this will help to desensitize him.

• When you go out, leave a radio or a TV on. Some dogs are comforted by hearing voices and background noise when they are left alone.

• Try to make your absences as short as possible when you are first training your dog to accept being on his own. When you return, do not fuss your dog, rushing to his crate to release him. Leave him for a few minutes, and when you go to him remain calm and relaxed so that he does not become hyped up with a huge greeting.

If you take these steps, your dog should become less anxious, and, over a period of time, you should be able to solve the problem. However, if you are failing to make progress, do not delay in calling in expert help.

challenge your authority. As we have seen, adolescent dogs test the boundaries, and this is the time to enforce all your earlier training so your Springer accepts that he is not top dog.

Springers were bred to be biddable, but they are clever dogs, and males, in particular, may become assertive as they mature. This often happens if early training has been neglected, or if you have allowed your adolescent Springer to rule the roost. Problems may also occur if you have taken on a rescued dog who has not been trained and socialised.

Assertive behaviour is expressed in many different ways, which may include the following:

- Showing lack of respect for your personal space. For example, your dog will barge through doors ahead of you or jump up at you.
- Getting up on to the sofa or your favourite armchair, and growling when you tell him to get back on the floor.
- Becoming possessive over a toy, or guarding his food bowl by growling when you get too close.
- Growling when anyone approaches his bed or when anyone gets too close to where he is lying.
- Ignoring basic obedience commands.
- Showing no respect to younger members of the family, pushing amongst them, and completely ignoring them.
- Male dogs may start marking (cocking their leg) in the house.

- Aggression towards people (see page 112).

If you see signs of your Springer becoming overly assertive, you must work at lowering his status so that he realises that you are the leader and he must accept your authority. Although you need to be firm, you also need to use positive training methods so that your Springer is rewarded for the behaviour you want. In this way, his 'correct' behaviour will be strengthened and repeated.

There are a number of steps you can take to lower your Springer's status. They include:

- Go back to basics and hold daily training sessions. Make sure you have some really tasty treats, or find a toy your Springer really values and only bring it out at training sessions. Run through all the training exercises you have taught your Springer. Make a big fuss of him and reward him when he does well. This will reinforce the message that you are the leader and that it is rewarding to do as you ask.
- Teach your Springer something new; this can be as simple as learning a trick, such as shaking paws. Having something new to think about will mentally stimulate your Springer, and he will benefit from interacting with you.
- Be 100 per cent consistent with all house rules – your Springer must never sit on the sofa, and you must never allow him to jump up at you.
- If your Springer has been guarding his food bowl, put the bowl down empty, and drop in a little food at a time. Periodically stop dropping in

A dominant dog may try to assert himself by taking over the sofa.

Channel your Springer's energies into games and training exercises so you can reward desirable behaviour.

the food, and tell your Springer to "Sit" and "Wait". Give it a few seconds, and then reward him by dropping in more food. This shows your Springer that you are the provider of the food, and he can only eat when you allow him to.

• Make sure the family eats before you feed your Springer. Some trainers advocate eating in front of the dog (maybe just a few bites from a biscuit) before starting a training session, so the dog appreciates your elevated status.

• Do not let your Springer barge through doors ahead of you, or leap from the back of the car before you release him. You may need to put your dog on the lead and teach him to "Wait" at doorways, and then reward him for letting you go through first.

If your Springer is progressing well with his retraining programme, think about getting involved with a dog sport, such as agility or competitive obedience. This will give your Springer a positive outlet for his energies. However, if your Springer is still trying to be

assertive, or you have any other concerns, do not delay in seeking the help of an animal behaviourist.

AGGRESSION

Aggression is a complex issue, as there are different causes and the behaviour may be triggered by numerous factors. It may be directed towards people, but far more commonly it is directed towards other dogs. Aggression in dogs may be the result of:

• Assertive behaviour (see page 109).
• Defensive behaviour: This may be induced by fear, pain or punishment.
• Territory: A dog may become aggressive if strange dogs or people enter his territory (which is generally seen as the house and garden).
• Intra-sexual issues: This is aggression between sexes – male-to-male or female-to-female.
• Parental instinct: A mother dog may become aggressive if she is protecting her puppies.

A dog who has been well socialised (see page 103) and has been given sufficient exposure to other dogs at significant stages of his development will rarely be aggressive. A well-bred Springer that has been reared correctly should not have a hint of aggression in his temperament. Obviously if you have taken on an older, rescued dog, you will have little or no knowledge of his background, and if he shows

GOOD CITIZEN SCHEME

This is a scheme run by the Kennel Club in the UK and the American Kennel Club in the USA. The schemes promote responsible ownership and help you to train a well-behaved dog who will fit in with the community. The schemes are excellent for all pet owners, and they are also a good starting point if you plan to compete with your Springer when he is older. The KC and the AKC schemes vary in format. In the UK there are three levels: bronze, silver and gold, with each test becoming progressively more demanding. In the AKC scheme there is a single test.

Some of the exercises in the scheme include:

- Walking on a loose lead among people and other dogs.
- Recall amid distractions.

- A controlled greeting where dogs stay under control while owners meet.
- The dog allows all-over grooming and handling by its owner, and also accepts being handled by the examiner.
- Stays, with the owner in sight, and then out of sight.
- Food manners, allowing the owner to eat without begging, and taking a treat on command.
- Sendaway – sending the dog to his bed.

The tests are designed to show the control you have over your dog, and his ability to respond correctly and remain calm in all situations. The Good Citizen Scheme is taught at most training clubs. For more information, log on to the Kennel Club or AKC website (see Appendices).

signs of aggression, the cause will need to be determined. In most cases, you would be well advised to call in professional help if you see aggressive behaviour in your dog; if the aggression is directed towards people, you should seek immediate advice. This behaviour can escalate very quickly and could lead to disastrous consequences.

NEW CHALLENGES

If you enjoy training your Springer, you may want to try one of the many dog sports that are now on offer.

SHOWING

In your eyes, your Springer is the most beautiful dog in the world – but would a judge agree? Showing is a highly competitive sport and as the Springer is so popular, classes tend to be very big. However, many owners are bitten by the showing bug, and their calendar is governed by the dates of the top showing fixtures.

To be successful in the show ring, a Springer must conform as closely as possible to the Breed Standard, which is a written blueprint describing the 'perfect' Springer (see Chapter Seven). To

get started you need to buy a puppy that has show potential and then train him to perform in the ring. A Springer will be expected to stand in show pose, gait for the judge in order to show off his natural movement, and to be examined by the judge. This involves a detailed hands-on examination, so your Springer must be bombproof when handled by strangers.

Many training clubs hold ringcraft classes, which are run by experienced showgoers. At these classes, you will learn how to handle your Springer in the

Showing is highly competitive, but very rewarding if you reach the top.

ring, and you will also find out about rules, procedures and show ring etiquette.

The best plan is to start off at some small, informal shows where you can practise and learn the tricks of the trade before graduating to bigger shows. It's a long haul starting in the very first puppy class, but the dream is to make your Springer up into a Show Champion.

COMPETITIVE OBEDIENCE

Border Collies and German Shepherds dominate this sport, but gundogs have also made their mark at the highest level. The Springer has the intelligence to do well in competitive obedience; the challenge is subduing the Springer's natural exuberance and producing the accuracy that is demanded. The classes start off being relatively easy and become progressively more challenging with additional exercises, and the handler giving minimal instructions to the dog.

Exercises include:

- Heelwork: Dog and handler must complete a set pattern on and off the lead, which includes left turns, right turns, about turns, and changes of pace.
- Recall: This may be when the handler is stationary or on the move.
- Retrieve: This may be a dumbbell or any article chosen by the judge.
- Sendaway: The dog is sent to a designated spot and must go into an instant Down until he is recalled by the handler.
- Stays: The dog must stay in the Sit and in the Down for a set amount of time. In advanced classes, the handler is out of sight.
- Scent: The dog must retrieve a single cloth from a pre-arranged pattern of cloths that has his owner's scent, or, in advanced classes, the judge's scent. There may also be decoy cloths.
- Distance control. The dog must execute a series of moves (Sit, Stand, Down) without moving from his position and with the handler at a distance.

Even though competitive obedience requires accuracy and precision, make sure you make it fun for your Springer, with lots

Agility is a fun sport for both dog and handler.

of praise and rewards so that you motivate him to do his best. Many training clubs run advanced classes for those who want to compete in obedience, or you can hire the services of a professional trainer so you can have one-on-one sessions.

AGILITY

This fun sport has grown enormously in popularity over the past few years. If you fancy having a go, make sure you have good control over your Springer and keep him slim. Agility is a very physical sport, which demands fitness from both dog and handler. A fat Springer is never going to make it as an agility competitor.

In agility competitions, each dog must complete a set course over a series of obstacles, which include:

- Jumps (upright hurdles and long jump)
- Weaves
- A-frame
- Dog walk
- Seesaw
- Tunnels (collapsible and rigid)
- Tyre

Dogs may compete in jumping classes with jumps, tunnels and weaves, or in agility classes, which have the full set of equipment. Faults are awarded for poles down on the jumps, missed contact points on the A-frame, dog walk and seesaw, and refusals. If a dog takes the wrong course, he is eliminated. The winner is the dog that completes

the course in the fastest time with no faults. As you progress up the grades, courses become progressively harder with more twists, turns and changes of direction.

If you want to get involved in agility, you will need to find a club that specialises in the sport (see Appendices). You will not be allowed to start training until your Springer is 12 months old, and you cannot compete until he is 18 months old. This rule is for the protection of the dog, who may suffer injury if he puts strain on bones and joints while he is still growing.

FIELD TRIALS

This is a sport where the Springer excels, as it tests his natural working ability. There is now a split between working Springers and show Springers, and if you are interested in competing in field trials, you will need a Springer that is bred from working lines.

In field trials, dogs are trained to work in an entirely natural environment. Nothing is set up, staged or artificial. The dogs may be asked to retrieve shot game from any type of terrain, including swamp, thick undergrowth and from water. They also need to perform blind retrieves, where they are sent out to find shot game when they haven't seen it fall. Dogs are judged on their natural game-finding abilities, their work in the shooting field, and their response to their handler. The two most crucial elements are steadiness and obedience.

Springers are built for this demanding job, with their waterproof coat, athletic physique and their great swimming ability. The other great plus factor is that Springers love to work closely with their handlers, so, if you put in the training, you could get to the top levels and even make your Springer into a field trial Champion.

If you are not aiming for the dizzy heights of making up a field trial Champion, you can test your Cocker Spaniel's working ability with the Gundog Working Certificate, which examines basic hunting and retrieving skills in the field. If a show Champion gains a Gundog Working Certificate, he can become a full Champion.

WORKING TRIALS

This is a very challenging sport, but the Springer Spaniel, with his excellent sense of smell, can be very successful. The sport consists of three basic components:

- Control: Dog and handler must complete obedience exercises, but the work does not have to be as precise as it is in competitive obedience. In the advanced classes, manwork (where the dog works as a guard/protection dog) is a major feature.

An English Springer competing in field trials is tested on his game-finding ability, his overall work in the shooting fields, and his response to his handler.

FLYBALL

Springers are natural retrievers, so they can be easily trained to be flyball competitors. Flyball is a team sport; the dogs love it, and it is undoubtedly the nosiest of all the canine sports!

Four dogs are selected to run in a relay race against an opposing team. The dogs are sent out by their handlers to jump four hurdles, catch the ball from the flyball box, and then return over the hurdles. At the top level, this sport is fast and furious, and although it is dominated by Border Collies, reliable Springers can make a big contribution. This is particularly true in multibreed competitions where the team is made up of four dogs of different breeds, and only one can be a Border Collie or a Working Sheepdog. Points are awarded to dogs and teams. Annual awards are given to top dogs and top teams, and milestone awards are given out to dogs as they attain points throughout their flyballing careers.

- Agility: The dog must negotiate a 3ft (0.91m) hurdle, a 9ft (2.75m) long jump, and a 6ft (1.82m) upright scale, which is the most taxing piece of dog equipment.
- Nosework: The dog must follow a track that has been laid over a set course. The surface may vary, and the length of time between the track being laid and the dog starting work is increased in the advanced classes.

The ladder of stakes are: Companion Dog, Utility Dog, Working Dog, Tracking Dog and Patrol Dog. In the US, tracking is a sport in its own right, and is very popular among Springer owners.

If you want to get involved in working trials, you will need to find a specialist club or a trainer that specialises in training for this sport.

DANCING WITH DOGS

This sport is relatively new, but it is becoming increasingly popular. It is very entertaining to watch, but it is certainly not as simple as it looks. To perform a choreographed routine to music with your Springer demands a huge amount of training.

Dancing with dogs is divided into two categories: heelwork to music and canine freestyle. In heelwork to music, the dog must work closely with his handler and show a variety of close 'heelwork' positions. In canine freestyle, the routine can be more flamboyant, with the dog working at a distance from the handler and performing spectacular tricks. Routines are judged on style and presentation, content and accuracy.

SUMMING UP

The Springer Spaniel is the great all-rounder of the canine world: he is a top-class working gundog, a glamorous show dog, and, most important of all, a wonderful companion. He has an outstanding temperament, and he is fun and rewarding to live with. Make sure you keep your half of the bargain: spend time socialising and training your Springer so that you can be proud to take him anywhere and he will always be a credit to you.

THE PERFECT ENGLISH SPRINGER

Chapter 7

here is no such thing as a perfect dog, even the wonderful English Springer Spaniel cannot make this claim, but there is a 'Standard' against which the breed can be measured.

WHAT IS A BREED STANDARD?

To capture the essence of the breed we must look to what is known as the Breed Standard. A Breed Standard is a written, descriptive set of guidelines detailing what the ideal character, temperament, purpose, shape, movement and colour should be for a particular breed of dog. It is to this ideal that all dogs are measured when being judged in the show ring. It was originally intended, as far as English Springers are concerned, to be a 'pattern' or blueprint for all dogs of this breed, whether they were intended for exhibition, as a working gundog, or as a pet. There is no such thing as a perfect dog, of course – even one who wins Best in Show at Crufts. Furthermore, there can be different interpretations of the guidelines when judging, which explains why the same dog does not win at every show and why one dog does not look exactly the same as another.

In 1934, some time after the breed had been introduced to the show ring in the UK, the English Springer Spaniel Clubs of England, Scotland and Wales approved the first Breed Standard. It was revised further in 1969. In 1982, the Kennel Club in the UK took responsibility for all Breed Standards. Many were standardised and shortened in 1989. Today, the Kennel Club holds the copyright for all Breed Standards covering all Kennel Club-recognised breeds. Any modification it might wish to make to a Standard in the future would be made in consultation with all the breed clubs concerned. The latest change was made in 2008, when the Kennel Club introduced the 'fit for purpose' clause to every Breed Standard, stating that: "*Breeders and judges should at all times be careful to avoid obvious conditions or exaggerations which would be detrimental in any way to the health, welfare or soundness of this breed.*" It also adds that "*If a feature or quality is desirable it should only be present in the right measure.*"

In Europe, and in most other countries, the governing body responsible for Breed Standards is the Fédération Cynologique Internationale (FCI). All its Standards are taken from the country of origin, in our case the UK, so there is no essential difference. However, the American Breed Standard, approved by, and in the ownership of, the English

The English Springer Spaniel Breed Standard is the blueprint for judging conformation, coat, colour, movement and temperament.

Springer Spaniel Field Trial Association, is that used by the American Kennel Club (AKC). It is much more specific and detailed than the UK Standard. The differences between the Standards do not altogether account for the differences between American and British dogs, although presentation and the preference for very little ticking in American show dogs may explain some of them. The AKC Standard is included here for comparison.

The original Breed Standard for English Springer Spaniels was more detailed than the current one, given here, but it was still quite a bare outline and open to considerable variance in interpretation. I have added a fuller explanation to each section, incorporating some of the earlier Standard and pointing out minor differences between the UK Standard and that used in the United States.

INTERPRETING BREED STANDARDS

GENERAL APPEARANCE
UK
Symmetrically built, compact, strong, merry, active. Highest on leg and raciest in build of all British land Spaniels.

AKC
The English Springer Spaniel is a medium-sized sporting dog, with a compact body and a docked tail. His coat is moderately long, with feathering on his legs, ears, chest and brisket. His pendulous ears, soft gentle expression, sturdy build and friendly wagging tail proclaim him unmistakably a member of the ancient family of Spaniels. He is above all a well-proportioned dog, free from exaggeration, nicely balanced in every part. His carriage is proud and upstanding, body deep, legs strong and muscular, with enough length to carry him with ease. Taken as a whole, the English Springer Spaniel suggests power, endurance and agility. He looks

the part of a dog who can go, and keep going, under difficult hunting conditions. At his best, he is endowed with style, symmetry, balance and enthusiasm and is every inch a sporting dog of distinct Spaniel character, combining beauty and utility.

The English Springer belongs to the spaniel family, which includes the American Cocker, Cocker, Clumber, Field, Sussex and Welsh Springer and is included within the 29 breeds that make up the gundog group. All are classed as land spaniels, although he will retrieve from, and enjoy being in, water. Missing from the above description is the earlier 'built for

endurance' phrase, which demonstrates that this is a dog that is not only balanced, strong and in a convenient package, but also must be capable of great stamina and look as if he can keep going all day – whatever the terrain or weather conditions. His happy outlook on life, and his ability to get on with all, has made him one of the most popular family pets.

CHARACTERISTICS
UK
Breed is of ancient and pure origins, oldest of sporting gundogs; original purpose was finding and springing game for net, falcon or greyhound. Now used to find, flush and retrieve game for gun.

The English Springer Spaniel is the 'Jack of all trades'. He is the perfect, all-round, working companion who can do every job a dog might be asked to do on a shoot. He is fearless in his approach to dense cover, and his scenting and hunting abilities are second to none. He can retrieve tenderly to hand and is a responsive dog that is eager to please. He is a pleasure to train. These qualities can be harnessed in many different directions to the Springer's traditional role as a gundog.

TEMPERAMENT
UK
Friendly, happy disposition, biddable. Timidity or aggression highly undesirable.

The English Springer is strong and compact, built on symmetrical lines.

ENGLISH SPRINGER SPANIEL

AKC

The typical Springer is friendly, eager to please, quick to learn and willing to obey. Such traits are conducive to tractability, which is essential for appropriate handler control in the field. In the show ring, he should exhibit poise and purpose and attentiveness and permit himself to be examined by the judge without resentment or cringing. Aggression toward people and aggression toward other dogs is not in keeping with sporting dog character and purpose is not acceptable. Excessive timidity, with due allowance for puppies and novice exhibits, is to be equally penalized.

Springers love people – both adults and children – and enjoy the company of other dogs. They also love life, and this makes them such a joy to own. You can forgive slight nervousness in a very young puppy in a new situation, but the right environment and socialisation should quickly produce a dog of very sound nature. However, if treated harshly, any dog may develop traits uncharacteristic of the breed. In the show ring a judge may well dismiss a dog that exhibits either timidity or aggression to people or other dogs.

HEAD AND SKULL
UK

Skull of medium length, fairly broad, slightly rounded, rising from foreface, making a brow or stop, divided by fluting between eyes, dying away along forehead towards occipital bone, which should not be prominent. Cheeks flat. Foreface of proportionate length to skull, fairly broad and deep, well chiselled below eyes, fairly deep and square in flew. Nostrils well developed.

AKC

The head is impressive without being heavy. Its beauty lies in a combination of strength and refinement. It is important that its size and proportion be in balance with the rest of the dog. Viewed in profile, the head appears approximately the same length as the neck and blends with the body in substance. The stop, eyebrows and chiseling of the bony structure around the eye sockets contribute to the Springer's beautiful and

A happy, out-going temperament is a hallmark of the breed.

characteristic expression, which is alert, kindly and trusting.

The skull is medium-length and fairly broad, flat on top and slightly rounded at the sides and back. The occiput bone is inconspicuous. As the skull rises from the foreface, it makes a stop, divided by a groove, or fluting, between the eyes. The groove disappears as it reaches the middle of the forehead. The amount of stop is moderate. It must not be a pronounced feature; rather it is a subtle rise where the muzzle joins the upper head. It is emphasized by the groove and by the position and shape of the eyebrows, which are well developed.

The muzzle is approximately the same length as the skull and one-half the width of the skull. Viewed in profile, the toplines of the skull and muzzle lie in approximately parallel planes. The nasal bone is straight, with no inclination downward towards the tip of the nose, the latter giving an undesirable 'down faced' look. Neither is the nasal bone concave, resulting in a 'dish-faced' profile; nor convex, giving the dog a Roman nose.

The cheeks are flat, and the face is well-chiseled under the eyes. Jaws are of sufficient length to allow the dog to carry game easily; fairly square, lean and strong. The upper lips come down full and rather square to cover the line of the lower jaw, however, the lips are never pendulous or exaggerated.

The soft, trusting expression that is so typical of the English Springer Spaniel.

The nose is fully-pigmented, liver or black in color, depending on the color of the coat. The nostrils are well-opened and broad.

The first thing you see when you look at an English Springer is its beautiful head, with a medium-length skull that is slightly flatter on top and rounded at the side and back, with no protruding bone at the occiput. Where the skull rises from the foreface above the muzzle there is a very moderate stop, and a groove or 'fluting' between the eyes that gradually disappears as it reaches the middle of the forehead. This makes the eyebrows well defined but not overly heavy. There should be a delicate moulding underneath the eyes that adds refinement to the head. The muzzle should be about the same length as the skull and roughly half its width. The nasal bone should be straight and, when viewed from the side, both the top of the skull and the top of the muzzle should be on seemingly parallel planes. The nose should be fully pigmented, either black or brown, to tone with the coat colour. The nostrils should be broad and well opened, allowing the good intake of air. A butterfly nose (i.e. one without full pigmentation) is not ideal but would not be as severely penalised in the UK as it would in the US.

EYES
UK
Medium size, almond-shaped, not prominent nor sunken, well set in (not showing haw), alert, kind expression. Dark hazel. Light eyes undesirable.

AKC
The eyes, more than any other feature, are the essence of the Springer's appeal. Correct size, placement and color influence expression and attractiveness. The eyes are of medium size and oval in shape, set rather well-apart and fairly deep in their sockets. The color of the iris harmonizes with the color of the coat, preferably dark hazel in the liver and white dogs and black or deep brown in the black and white dogs. Eye rims are fully pigmented and match the coat in colour. Lids are tight with little or no haw showing. Eyes that are

small, round or protruding, as well as eyes that are yellow or brassy in colour, are highly undesirable.

The eye and expression is the essence of an English Springer. It is soft and trusting, yet intelligent. These ingredients are altered if the size and shape is not correct or if the colour is too light. The eyes should be deeply set within the socket and reasonably wide apart. A round or protruding eye would give an atypical look and a completely different expression. We would expect the iris to be dark hazel in a liver-and-white dog but this would deepen to a brown or dark brown in a black-and-white dog, although it may be slightly lighter where there is a tri-coloured coat. Green or brassy yellow eyes are atypical, but a slighter lighter eye on a young puppy may well darken with time, particularly if the iris is encircled with a darker ring. The American Standard states that the eye rims should be fully pigmented and match the coat colour. This is understood in the UK, although it is not stated in the Standard. Both the UK and American Standards agree that the eye rim should be tight (not showing haw) to avoid the possibility of infection caused by invasive objects like grass seeds.

EARS
UK
Lobular, good length and width, fairly close to head, set in line with eye. Nicely feathered.

AKC
Ears are long and fairly wide, hanging close to the cheeks with no tendency to stand up or out. The ear leather is thin and approximately long enough to reach the tip of the nose. Correct ear set is on a level with the eye and not too far back on the skull.

The ears are fairly wide and of thin leather, being approximately long enough to reach the tip of the nose. They should not stand up or out but hang close to the side of the head and be set fairly low on the head in line with the outer corner of the eye. They should not be so long as to interfere with the ability to move quickly and easily when scenting. The ear is one area of a spaniel that needs to be looked after carefully and it should be cleaned regularly. Its pendulous shape can trap moisture within, making it more prone to infection. The feathering should be kept well combed to avoid heavy matting and can be trimmed under the ear to allow more air to circulate within the ear passage.

MOUTH
KC
Jaws strong, with a perfect, regular and complete scissor bite, i.e. upper teeth closely overlapping lower teeth and set square to the jaws.

AKC
Teeth are strong, clean, of good size and ideally meet in a close scissors bite. An even bite or

IN THE RING

Every dog is given a hands-on examination by the judge.

The judge will assess movement from the front, from the rear, and in profile.

one of two incisors slightly out of line are minor faults. **Undershot, overshot and wry jaws are serious faults and are to be severely penalized.**

The jaws should be strong and large enough to be able to carry game easily and fairly square, with the flews or lips sufficient to cover the lower jaw but not exaggerated nor pendulous. An even bite (where top and bottom teeth meet exactly), undershot (where the bottom jaw overlaps the top jaw), overshot (where the top jaw overlaps the bottom jaw) or wry jaw (when one side of the jaw has grown more than the other, so that the teeth may meet correctly on the left side, but not on the right, for example) would be heavily penalised in the show ring, although it would not necessarily interfere with a dog's retrieving ability.

The neck must be strong and muscular so the Springer is able to retrieve game.

NECK

UK

Good length, strong and muscular, free from throatiness, slightly arched, tapering towards head.

AKC

The neck is moderately long, muscular, clean and slightly arched at the crest. It blends gradually and smoothly into sloping shoulders. The portion of the topline from withers to tail is firm and slopes very gently.

The emphasis here is in strength, which is necessary for the English Springer to do his job

properly, to hold his nose just above the ground when moving, and to support the head and jaws when retrieving a heavy object. The original Standard asked for the neck to be 'well set into the shoulders and nicely arched, tapering towards the head to give great activity and speed'. A neck that is too short would interfere with the dog's retrieving ability, and, equally, if the neck were too long, it would lose some of its strength. It is generally accepted that the length of neck should be approximately equal to the length of head. Loose folds of skin on the throat would be more prone to catch on twigs

and branches, causing injury as well as being unsightly.

FOREQUARTERS

UK

Forelegs straight and well boned. Shoulders sloping and well laid. Elbows set well to body. Strong flexible pasterns.

AKC

Efficient movement in front calls for proper forequarter assembly. The shoulder blades are flat, fairly close together at the tips, molding smoothly into the contour of the body. Ideally, when measured from the top of the withers to the point of the shoulder to the

elbow, the shoulder blade and upper arm of apparent equal length, forming an angle of nearly 90 degrees; this sets the front legs well under the body and places the elbows directly beneath the tips of the shoulder blades. Elbows lie close to the body. Forelegs are straight with the same degree of size continuing to the foot. Bone is strong, slightly flattened, not too round or too heavy. Pasterns are short, strong and slightly sloping, with no suggestion of weakness. Dewclaws are usually removed.

The leg bone should be of sufficient strength to carry the body and is generally seen as 'flat round' in shape. The shoulder blade should be flat and meet the upper arm at an angle of approximately 90 degrees, both bones being of roughly even length, setting the legs well under the body, and the elbows beneath the shoulders and lying flat against the body. The legs should be straight, and the feet should neither point inwards or outwards.

BODY
UK
Strong, neither too long nor too short. Chest deep, well developed. Well-sprung ribs. Loin muscular, strong with slight arch and well coupled.

AKC
The body is short-coupled, strong and compact. The chest is deep, reaching the level of the elbows, with well-developed forechest; however, it is not so wide or round as to interfere with the action of the front legs. Ribs are fairly long, springing gradually to the middle of the body, then tapering as they approach the end of the ribbed section. The underline stays level with the elbows to a slight upcurve at the flank. The back is straight, strong and essentially level. Loins are strong, short and slightly arched. Hips are nicely-rounded, blending smoothly into the hind legs. The croup slopes gently to the set of the tail, and tail-set follows the natural line of the croup.

The body should be slightly longer than the length of leg.

An undocked tail should be well feathered, and should be in balance with the rest of the dog.

This is the 'engine room' of the dog and produces the stamina called for in the field. The body should be just slightly longer than the length of leg and yet appears quite compact. The chest should have depth, rather than excessive width, so as to give plenty of heart room but not impede the function and straightness of the forelimbs. The good spring of the ribs allows great lung capacity for endurance. The underline shows a slight arch at the abdomen. The topline, although not described officially, should be level, rounding slightly at the croup and down to the tail. The coupling refers to the distance between the ribs and the pelvis that should be reasonably short for strength, but long enough for flexibility, particularly in a bitch where it provides space for a litter.

HINDQUARTERS
UK
Hindlegs well let down. Stifles and hocks moderately bent. Thighs broad, muscular, well developed. Coarse hocks undesirable.

AKC
The Springer should be worked and shown in hard, muscular condition with well-developed hips and thighs. His whole rear assembly suggests strength and driving power. Thighs are broad and muscular. Stifle joints are strong. For functional efficiency, the angulation of the hindquarter is never greater than that of the forequarter, and not appreciably less. The hock joints are somewhat rounded, not small and sharp in contour. Rear pasterns are short (about one-third the distance from the hip joints to the foot) and strong, with good bone. When viewed from behind, the rear pasterns are parallel. Dewclaws are usually removed .

Propulsion comes mostly from the hindquarters and is the result of a combination of correctly fitting ball-and-socket joints at the hips, adequate length of bone, and moderate angulation to match the forequarters at the stifle (knee) and hock joints. A shorter distance between the hock joint (which should be rounded) and the floor provides greater drive. The first and second thigh muscles should be broad and well conditioned to achieve effortless, yet economic, movement. Cow hocks (where the knee joint is slightly misaligned, resulting in feet spaying outwards) or sickle hocks (where a

When a Springer is moving, the tail should be carried horizontally, never above the level of the back.

misaligned knee joint results in the lower leg being set too far forward so that leg does not appear straight) are undesirable.

FEET

UK
Tight, compact, well rounded, with strong, full pads.

AKC
Front: Feet are round or slightly oval. They are compact and well-arched, of medium size, with thick pads, and well-feathered between the toes. Rear: The feet are the same as in front, except that they are smaller and often more compact.

The front feet bear most of the dog's weight so tend to be slightly larger than those at the rear. We often refer to them as being cat-like, with good shock absorbance, and yet flexible enough to negotiate rough terrain. Nails should be kept short and any dewclaws removed to avoid damage when working. Interestingly, the AKC Standard describes the feet as 'webbed'.

TAIL

UK
Previously customarily docked. Docked: set low, never carried above level of back. Well feathered with lively action. Undocked: set low, never carried above level of back. Well feathered with lively action. In balance with the rest of the dog.

AKC
The tail is carried horizontally or slightly elevated and displays a characteristic lively, merry action, particularly when the dog is on game. A clamped tail **(indicating timidity or undependable temperament) is to be faulted, as is a tail carried at a right angle to the backline in terrier fashion.**

Traditionally, the tail was docked to approximately two-thirds of its original length to minimise the risk of injury when working in heavy cover. The fine tip is particularly vulnerable and can catch easily. For this reason, the UK government has made an exemption for working gundogs in its decision to ban the docking of tails under the terms of the Animal Welfare Act, effective in England from 6 April 2007, Wales from 28 March 2007. This exemption does not apply in Scotland, where the Scottish parliament has implemented a total ban on the docking of tails from 31 April 2007. No dog bred after this time and sporting a docked tail will be allowed to compete in a show ring where the general public has to pay an entrance fee. A similar ban is already effective in some European countries.

The tail, regardless of length, should be set reasonably low and not carried above the back, although this is sometimes forgiven in an excitable, young male and is definitely preferable to one that carries its tail right down, as this indicates timidity. Its lively action reflects the dog's happy temperament and is a joy to see. The American Standard allows a 'slightly elevated' tail carriage, although not as upright as in a terrier.

GAIT/MOVEMENT
UK
Strictly his own. Forelegs swing straight forward from the shoulder, throwing feet well forward in an easy, free manner. Hocks driving well under body, following in line with forelegs. At slow movement may have a pacing stride typical of this breed.

AKC
The final test of the Springer's conformation and soundness is proper movement. Balance is the prerequisite to good movement. The front and rear assemblies must be equivalent in angulation and muscular development for the gait to be smooth and effortless.

Shoulders which are well laid-back to permit a long stride are just as essential as the excellent rear quarters that provide driving power. Seen from the side, the Springer exhibits a long ground-covering stride and carries a firm back, with no tendency to dip, roach or roll from side to side. From the front, the legs swing forward in a free and easy manner. Elbows have free action from the shoulders, and the legs show no tendency to cross or interfere. From behind, the rear legs reach well under the body, following on a line with the forelegs. As speed increases, there is a natural tendency for the legs to converge toward a center line of travel. Movement faults include high-stepping, wasted motion; short, choppy stride; crabbing; and moving with the feet wide, the latter giving roll or swing to the body.

Correct conformation should produce effortless movement that covers the ground with economy and style. When viewed from front or rear, the legs should be parallel and the topline should be held throughout. A straight shoulder will make for a choppy action in front, which is not typical.

Movement should be effortless and ground covering.

Although the pacing stride mentioned is common at slow movement, it is generally frowned upon in the show ring.

COAT

UK

Close, straight and weather resisting, never coarse. Moderate feathering on ears, forelegs, body and hindquarters.

AKC

The Springer has an outer coat and an undercoat. On the body, the outer coat is of medium length, flat or wavy and is easily distinguishable from the undercoat, which is short, soft and dense. The quantity of undercoat is affected by climate and season. When in combination, outer coat and undercoat serve to make the dog substantially waterproof, weatherproof and thornproof. On ear, chest, legs and belly the Springer is nicely furnished with a fringe of feathering of moderate length and heaviness. On the head, front of the forelegs, and below the hock joint on the font of the hind legs, the hair is short and fine. The coat has the clean, glossy, 'live' appearance indicative of good health. It is legitimate to trim about the head, ears, neck and feet, to remove dead undercoat, and to thin and shorten excess feathering as required to enhance a smart, functional appearance. The tail may be trimmed, or well-fringed with wavy feathering. Above all, the appearance should be natural. Overtrimming, especially of the body coat, or any chopped, barbered or artificial effect is to be penalized in the show ring, as is excessive feathering that destroys the clean outline desirable in a sporting dog. Correct quality and condition of coat is to take precedence over quantity of coat.

The English Springer should have both an undercoat and a topcoat. The undercoat provides both warmth in the winter and keeps the body insulated against heat in the summer. The topcoat is well oiled to shrug off water and gives that beautiful sheen. The coat moults according to the season and central heating has played its part in altering when this should be. In ideal kennel conditions the coat will be thick, but fine, in texture, lying flat against the body and requiring the minimum of maintenance. Exposure to the sun will bleach a liver-and-white coat but does not seem to affect the black-and-white to the same degree. The feathering varies according to thickness of coat but should not be so long as to

Tan markings on a liver and white Springer.

interfere with the dog's function as a gundog. It was originally intended to protect the more vulnerable areas from injury when working. In practice, the moderate feathering called for is slightly exaggerated in the show dog, particularly in America.

COLOUR
UK
Liver and white, black and white, or either of these colours with tan markings.

A black and white tricolour.

AKC
All of the following combinations of colors and markings are equally acceptable: (1) Black or liver with white markings or predominantly white with black or liver markings; (2) Blue or liver roan; (3) Tricolor: black and white or liver and white with tan markings, usually found on eyebrows, cheeks, inside of ears and under the tail. Any white portion of the coat may be flecked with ticking. Off colors, such as lemon, red or orange, are not to place.

There is no rule as to how much colour or white should be present in the body coat, and, theoretically, markings are not important. In practice, the majority of show-bred dogs have more colour than many seen in the field, and the classically marked dog will sport a solid-coloured jacket with a white collar and legs. The head and ears will be solid colour with a white blaze or flash rising from the muzzle to the forehead, and the muzzle and front of the neck will also be white. Any amount of ticking is allowed on the body, legs and muzzle. In a tri-coloured dog the tan will be present to a lesser or greater degree on the eyebrows, lower cheeks and under the tail, with tan spots amid theticking on the legs and muzzle.

SIZE/PROPORTION AND SUBSTANCE
UK
Approx. height: 51 cm (20 in).

AKC
The Springer is built to cover rough ground with agility and reasonable speed. His structure suggests the capacity for endurance. He is to be kept to medium size. Ideal height at the shoulder for dogs is 20 inches; for bitches, it is 19 inches. Those more than one inch under or over the breed ideal are to be faulted. A 20-inch dog, well proportioned and in good condition, will weigh approximately 50 pounds; a 19-inch bitch will weight approximately 40 pounds. The length of the body (measured from the point of shoulder to point of buttocks) is slightly greater than the height at the withers. The dog too long in body, especially when long in loin, tires easily and lacks the compact outline characteristic of the breed. A dog too short in body for the length of his legs, a condition which destroys balance and restricts gait, is equally undesirable. A Springer with correct substance appears well-knit and sturdy with good bone, however, is never coarse or ponderous.

The original UK Standard also mentioned an approximate weight of 50 lb (22.5 kg). It is generally accepted that most bitches will be slightly smaller at around 19-20 inches (48.5-51 cm) and correspondingly lighter than the males. In the UK, a male dog standing slightly taller than the height of the Standard would not be penalised, provided he was in proportion. This is spelled out in the American version, allowing one inch (2.5 cm) either side of the ideal for bitch and dog and a comparable weight for the bitch.

FAULTS

Any departure from the foregoing points should be considered a fault and the seriousness with which the fault should be regarded should be in exact proportion to its degree and its effect upon the health and welfare of the dog, and on the dog's ability to perform its traditional work.

In the US, faults are enumerated under various headings into serious, not so serious and not to place (disqualifying). In the UK this is for the judge to decide.

NOTE

Male animals should have two apparently normal testicles fully descended into the scrotum.

This is absent from the American Standard. In theory, in the UK it is now possible to exhibit neutered animals, provided permission has been granted by the Kennel Club. However, in practice, very few neutered males are shown.

SUMMARY

In evaluating the English Springer Spaniel, the overall picture is a primary consideration. One should look for type, which includes general appearance and outline, and also for soundness, which includes movement and temperament. Inasmuch as the dog with a smooth, easy gait must be reasonably sound and well balanced, he is to be highly regarded – however, not to the extent of forgiving him for not looking like an English Springer Spaniel. An atypical dog, too short or long in leg length, or foreign in head or expression, may move well, but he is not to be preferred over a good all-round specimen that has a minor fault in movement. It must be remembered that the English Springer Spaniel is first and foremost a sporting dog of the Spaniel family, and he must look, behave and move in character.

Win or lose – the best dog is the one you take home with you...

HAPPY AND HEALTHY

Chapter 8

In order to keep your Springer Spaniel healthy, he must be given regular walks and mental stimulation, he must be fed a balanced diet, and he must be provided with veterinary care, including vaccinations and parasite control.

Improved diet and routine vaccinations have resulted in a longer life expectancy for our pets, but the owner still has an important role to play in everyday health care. It is very important that you really get to know your dog, as you will more easily identify when the dog is 'off colour'. Visits to the vet should be made when anything unusual is detected. Pet insurance has allowed many owners to take advantage of the latest tests and treatments available, although it is important to check the policy for exclusions.

VACCINATIONS

One of the greatest advances in canine medicine in the last 50 years has been the development of effective vaccines. Within living memory dogs died from fits brought on by distemper, and in the last 20 years many puppies have died from parvovirus. The routine use of a multiple-component vaccine to protect against canine distemper, infectious canine hepatitis, parvovirus and leptospirosis has prevented many of these deaths.

Different vets have slightly different practices for administering vaccines. The age at which a puppy receives its first vaccine can vary. The timing for the primary vaccine course is based on an understanding of when the immunity provided by the puppy's mother declines to a level that will not interfere with the immune response. In the UK, it is normally recommended that

a puppy receives its final dose of the primary vaccine course at 10 or 12 weeks of age, and boosters after the first year are usual. The infection risk of various diseases varies across regions, so your vet, who will have local knowledge about disease risk and effective prevention measures, and can assess your dog's level of immunity, should schedule vaccination courses.

PARASITE CONTROL

There are two groups of parasites that can affect your English Springer – ectoparasites (those that live on the body, such as fleas) and endoparasites (those that live in the body, such as worms). Your vet will advise you on a necessary regime to control these parasites.

WORMING

Routine worming every three months is necessary, not only for

Spot-on treatments are effective against external parasites.

your dog's comfort, but also to reduce the risk of infection in humans handling the dog. Puppies should be wormed as well as adult dogs. There are a number of worms that affect dogs. The main ones are roundworm, hookworm, tapeworm and whipworm. Many worming treatments can destroy all of these with one treatment. Your vet will discuss a suitable product and regime with you.

FLEA CONTROL
Fleas are the biggest problem for dog owners, especially since fleas can cause irritating bites on humans as well as dogs. A single flea can cause persistent scratching and restlessness. Many effective anti-flea preparations are now available, some as tablets, some as coat applications and some as sprays to treat soft furnishings as well as affected animals.

OTHER ECTOPARASITES
Lice, fleas, and mites may all cause irritation or disease and are not easily visible to the eye. Ticks, however, become quite large and easy to spot as they gorge themselves on the dog's blood. A thorough grooming of the dog each day will detect many of these parasites and they can be destroyed and prevented with a variety of different products, including powders, shampoos, spot-on insecticides, or sprays. Collars impregnated with insecticides are less in favour.

DIET AND EXERCISE
It is a good idea to weigh all dogs on a regular basis and to keep records, including an account of the dog's food intake. Each dog should have an ideal weight, and, within a narrow range, the correct weight for the dog will act as a guide.

Obesity has become a major concern for dogs. Appetite suppressants can now be used: mitratapide (Yarvitan) can help as part of an overall weight-management programme. For further information, see Chapter 5 or consult your vet.

GROOMING
Grooming is covered in Chapter 5, but it is mentioned here because it plays an important part in preventative health care. Regular grooming not only stimulates skin and hair growth, but also provides an opportunity for the early detection of health problems.

During grooming sessions, attention should be paid to bony prominences, skin folds, feet and claws, eyes and ears, mouth and teeth, anus, vulva and prepuce, as well as to the skin and coat. The coat should be checked for fleas and ticks, and the ears must be examined both inside and out. Lip folds should be checked for excess saliva or unpleasant breath. Some of the spaniel breeds are more prone to eczema around the lips than other working breeds.

The pads of the feet should feel quite soft to the touch and not leathery or horny (hyperkeratinised). Check for cysts, swellings and inflammation between the toes. Warts are sometimes found on the feet of young dogs, especially those kept in kennels, where regular washing of the concrete runs leads to excessive wetting of the dog's feet.

The nails should be short and of even length. If the nails are too long, they need to be clipped. Dewclaws, if present, are not a disadvantage to the dog unless they have grown overlong or grown in a circle, penetrating the flesh and causing an infected wound.

A-Z OF COMMON AILMENTS

ALLERGIES

A frequent diagnosis for many dogs with skin and intestinal disorders, an allergy is the result of an inappropriate immune response by the dog to an antigen in food or inhaled through the nose. Working out the cause and eliminating it is the most effective course of treatment. Medication can also be used to suppress the allergic response.

ANAEMIA

Oxygen is carried throughout the body by haemoglobin in the red blood cells. Anaemia occurs when there is insufficient haemoglobin or red blood cells. Signs of anaemia include pale skin and gums (not always easy to see in a dog), loss of appetite, tiring on exercise, general weakness, rapid breathing with increased heart rate, and even collapse. Most cases of anaemia are regenerative, and a source of iron, either dietary or in tablet form, can help in the short-term. Antibiotics may be prescribed if an infection is responsible. In some cases a blood transfusion may be necessary.

ALOPECIA

Hair loss can be either in patches or total. The disorder is usually hormonal, associated with diseases that affect the hormone balance, such as hypothyroidism (Cushing's disease), or tumours affecting the reproductive organs. Treatment for alopecia is based on identifying and treating the underlying cause.

ANAL DISORDERS

Sacculitis: Modern diets are often blamed for the high incidence of dogs needing their anal glands squeezed out at regular intervals. These glands contain strong-smelling, greasy substances used to 'mark' the freshly passed faeces for other animals to recognise. Over-

production of the fluid may cause the dog to 'scoot' along the floor to relieve discomfort. Occasionally, infection also occurs, which can be treated with antibiotics. Abscesses of the anal sacs are very painful. They may require drainage, although they often swell and burst on their own. Flushing out and antibiotics may be necessary.

Ademomata: Benign tumours or cysts in the anal glands are found in the older male dog and require veterinary attention before bleeding occurs.

ARTHRITIS

Joint disease can occur after an infection, but it is usually due to joint wear and tear (degenerative) or an immune system reaction (rheumatoid arthritis and idiopathic arthritis). Dogs will show lameness in one or more joints and may tire on exercise.

Treatment involves keeping the dog mobile, controlling the dog's weight, and the prescription of anti-inflammatory medication on a daily basis to control pain. For your Springer's comfort provide soft, comfortable bedding and encourage frequent short walks.

ASCITES

Commonly known as 'dropsy', ascites is a condition where fluid builds up in the abdomen. It is often associated with chronic heart or liver disease and is most likely to be seen in the elderly Springer. The condition can be treated following a full veterinary inspection for underlying causes. Diuretics, cardiac, and liver drugs may also be used. Stress and exercise should be reduced, and diets with little salt and increased potassium and magnesium may be advised.

BRONCHITIS

Inflammation of the breathing tubes is often the result of a virus or a bacterial infection, but irritant gases and dust can also be the cause of repeated coughing. Kennel cough is the most common infection, which results in sticky mucus clinging to the base of the windpipe (trachea) and the tubes entering the lungs (bronchii). Coughing similar to bronchitis is seen in older dogs associated with congestive heart failure. Antibiotics may be prescribed by the vet to reduce the signs and the risk of further bacterial infection, leading to generalised pneumonia. Cough suppressants and 'antitussives' can be used to suppress a persistent cough, but should not be used if there is bronchopneumonia. Steam inhalations, often with a volatile oil, have been used to relieve a dry cough in Springers.

CALCULI (BLADDER STONES)

Calculi are deposits of mineral

TREATING BURNS AND SCALDS

First-aid measures for burns and scalds require immediate cooling of the skin, which can be done by pouring cold water over the affected part repeatedly for at least 10 minutes. Some scalds penetrate the coat and may not be recognised until a large area of skin and hair peels away. As these injuries are considered to be very painful, analgesics (pain relief) should be obtained, and, in anything but the smallest injured area, antibiotics are advisable. An Elizabethan collar may be used to prevent the Springer licking the area. In cases showing signs of shock, intravenous fluid therapy may be a necessity.

salts from the urine, either in the neck of the bladder or nearer the base of the penis in the male. Stones can also form in the kidneys and these cause pain as they enter the ureters.

Calculi are recognisable on X-ray or with ultrasound examinations. The obstruction may be partial or complete. The dog will strain, looking uncomfortable or in pain. An operation is usually needed to remove calculi, and dietary advice will be given on how to avoid further attacks. Increasing the dog's water intake and providing opportunities for frequent bladder emptying are equally important in prevention.

CANCER (CARCINOMA)

The frequency of cancer in Springers is no greater than in any other breed, but as dogs are now living longer, owners are more likely to be faced with a cancer diagnosis, particularly in the dog's later years. One in every four dogs will have one of the many types of cancer.

CATARACTS

Any opaqueness of the lens of the eye is termed a cataract, and it can result in blindness. Cataracts are commonly seen in older dogs or those with diabetes, but can occur in young dogs following an injury to the eye. Some breeds are affected with congenital cataracts, seen once the puppy opens its eyes. Once the condition has been diagnosed, cataract surgery, performed at specialised ophthalmic centres, is very successful in suitably selected cases.

CONSTIPATION

Unless the Springer is known to have consumed large quantities of bone or fibrous matter, straining may well be due to an enlarged prostate gland in the male, or any foreign body in the rectum. Increasing the fluid intake and the medication of liquid paraffin is advised, but if the problem persists, the vet should be consulted.

CRUCIATE LIGAMENT INJURY

The knee joint is a structure prone to injury in athletic dogs and it is now possible to have a total knee replacement operation in selected cases. There are two cruciate ligaments that hold the knee together. If one of these is torn as a result of jumping or a severe sprain, the stifle (knee joint) is destabilised with severe, sudden pain. This is most likely to occur in middle-aged, overweight Springers. A vet will normally advise surgical repair. If left untreated, chronic arthritis of the knee will result.

Regular exercise is a must for English Springer Spaniels – and their owners...

CYSTITIS

Inflammation of the bladder is more common in the bitch, and may first be noticed when the animal strains frequently, passing only small quantities of urine. Bacteria reaching the bladder from outside the body are the usual cause. In all cases the fluid intake should be reviewed, as a good 'wash through' of the bladder will reduce the risk of bacteria and mineral particles irritating the bladder lining. Medication with antispasmodics and an appropriate antibiotic will be required.

DIABETES

Dogs suffer from two types of diabetes, but the more common is 'sugar diabetes', known as DM (diabetes mellitus), which is seen more frequently in the older bitch. It is caused by a lack of insulin to regulate the level of glucose in the blood. The signs of increased thirst, passing large quantities of urine, eye cataracts and muscle weakness are associated with increased appetite and weight loss as the dog attempts to satisfy the variations of his sugar levels. Diagnosis by urine and blood samples is followed by the injection of insulin once or more daily.

Diabetes insipidus is uncommon in dogs and is related to the water-control mechanism of the kidneys.

DISTEMPER

Fortunately, distemper is now rare. Routine vaccination has been very effective in preventing disease, but there is always the threat of a Springer acquiring the infection if there has been a breakdown in the immune system. Affected dogs develop a high temperature, cough, diarrhoea, and a purulent eye discharge. After several weeks, further complications, such as pneumonia or damage to the nerve system, may set in.

EPILEPSY AND FITS

Seizures occur relatively commonly in dogs and represent an acute, and usually brief, disturbance of normal electrical activity in the brain. However, it is distressing for both the patient and the owner. Most fits last only a short time (less than two minutes), and owners often telephone for veterinary advice once the seizure is over. Fits can sometimes occur close together. Following a fit, a vet should examine the dog, even if the seizure has stopped. Medication is used to control fits, but long-term treatment may be needed.

EYE PROBLEMS

Conjunctivitis is common in Springer Spaniels and other breeds that go out in grass. The signs of a red eye with a watery or crusty discharge are easy to recognise. Chemicals and allergies cause irritation, but a presentation of acute, severe conjunctivitis may indicate the presence of a foreign body, such as a grass seed, under the eyelids. Careful examination of the inner surfaces of both eyelids, and the third eyelid, is necessary to identify and remove foreign material. Another cause of conjunctivitis is the inturning of the edge of the eyelid, known as entropion.

There are other eye disorders, such as corneal ulcers, keratitis and 'dry eye' (KCS), that require specific veterinary attention.

FRACTURES

Most broken bones are the result of injury. An old dog with kidney disease may have brittle bones, but spontaneous fractures are quite rare. Treatment of fractures will require the immediate attention of the vet. There is little point in attempting first aid, as the Springer will be in pain and will adopt the most comfortable position he can find. Natural painkillers, known as endorphins,

come into action immediately following such an injury. If there is a skin wound associated with the fracture, it should be covered to reduce bacterial contamination. X-rays will be necessary to confirm a crack or a major displacement of bones.

HEART AND CARDIAC DISORDERS

Heart disease may show itself in many forms, affecting many dogs from young puppies through to the ageing Springer. Disease in young dogs may be congenital, while reduced exercise and weight increase in the older dog are contributory factors to a failing heart. Medication has improved tremendously in recent years and can give a good long-term prognosis.

HEARTWORM DISEASE

Heartworms are becoming more common in the UK but are a

major problem in the USA where they are spread by mosquitoes. The filarial worms live in the heart and blood vessels of the lungs and cause signs such as tiring, exercise intolerance and a soft, deep cough. Dogs may be protected from six to eight weeks of age with a monthly dose of the medication advised by the vet. There are a number of products available. A blood test can be used to see if the heartworm antigen is present.

HEPATITIS

Inflammation of the liver may be due to a virus, but it is uncommon in dogs that have been protected with vaccines that also prevent the bacteria Leptospira damaging the liver.

Chronic liver disease may be due to heart failure, tumours or some type of toxicity. Dietary treatment may help if there are no specific medicines to use. The skin condition known as hepato-cutaneous syndrome seems slightly more common in spaniel breeds. It may affect the feet with non-healing sores.

INTERVERTEBRAL DISC DISEASE AND PARALYSIS

Collapse or sudden weakness of the hindquarters may be due to pressure on the spinal nerves supplying the muscles and other sensory receptors. A 'slipped disc', as it is commonly known, may be responsible, but any injury to the spine, a fibro-cartilage embolism, a fracture, or a tumour, may cause similar paralysis. The signs include

Vaccination has had a huge impact on the spread of infectious diseases.

dragging one or both hind legs, lack of tail use, and often the loss of bladder and bowel control. X-rays, a neurological assessment and possibly an MRI scan will be needed to be certain of the cause. Some cases respond well to surgical correction, but medical treatment can also be effective and is less costly. Home-nursing care should include keeping the dog clean and groomed, help with bladder or bowel movement, and carrying out any physiotherapy advised by the vet.

JAUNDICE

Jaundice is recognisable by the yellowing of the skin and the whites of the eyes. It is caused by liver damage and retention of the yellow pigment from the breakdown of blood haemoglobin. Jaundice is usually accompanied by a loss of appetite and general disinterest in going for walks. Veterinary attention is urgent. With adequate treatment jaundice will disappear over a few weeks. Care must be taken to avoid further liver damage and some dogs may become carriers of infection. See also Leptospirosis.

KENNEL COUGH

The signs of kennel cough include a goose-honking cough, and hacking or retching that lasts for days to several weeks. It is

GASTRO-ENTERITIS

Vomiting is relatively common in dogs, and it can be a protective mechanism to prevent poisonous substances entering the body. Gastro-enteritis includes diarrhoea attacks, which is a similar process of getting rid of undesirable intestine contents by washing them out. The production of extra mucus and intestinal fluid is seen with a rapid bowel evacuation. Both products of gastro-enteritis are distressing to dog and owner alike. There are many causes, ranging from the dog needing worming to the complex interaction of viruses and bacteria.

Where the signs of gastro-enteritis last more than 48 hours, a vet should be prepared to take samples and test for a variety of diseases, such as pancreatitis, colitis or tumours, as some disorders may be life-threatening.

Treatment at home may be tried, stopping feeding for 48-72 hours, and allowing fluids in repeated, small quantities. Ice cubes in place of water in the bowl may help reduce vomiting. Electrolyte solutions will help with rehydration. Once signs are alleviated, small feeds of smooth foods, such as steamed fish or chicken with boiled rice, may be gradually introduced.

due to damage at the base of the windpipe and bronchial tubes. The dry, unproductive cough is caused by a combination of viruses, bacteria and Mycoplasma. Vaccination is helpful in preventing the disease but may not give full protection, as strains of kennel cough seem to vary. The disease is highly contagious and spread by

droplets, so it may be acquired at dog shows or boarding kennels. An incubation period of five to seven days is usual. Veterinary treatments alleviate the cough and reduce the duration of the illness.

LEPTOSPIROSIS

Dogs that live in the country or swim in water may be more prone to this infection. Leptospira bacteria carried by rats may be found in pools and ditches where rodents have visited. Annual vaccination against the two types of Leptospira is advised. Treatment in the early stages, using antibiotics, is effective, but liver and kidney damage may permanently incapacitate the Springer if the early signs and associated fever are not recognised. Kidney and liver failure will lead to death.

LYME DISEASE BORRELIOSIS

This tick-borne disease, which affects dogs, humans, and, to a lesser extent, other domestic animals, is common in the USA. It is estimated that there may be a thousand cases a year in the UK. Often, it is seen as a sudden lameness with a fever or, in the chronic form, one or two joints are affected with arthritis. Suspicion should be raised if a rash appears around the bite and quickly spreads.

Treatment for Lyme Disease is effective. Blood tests can confirm Borrelia at the laboratory.

NEPHRITIS

Dogs may suffer acute kidney failure after poisoning, obstructions to the bladder, or after shock with reduced blood supply. Chronic nephritis is more common in older dogs where the blood accumulates waste products that the damaged kidneys cannot remove. The syndrome is caused by immune-mediated damage within the kidney. The signs of increased thirst, loss of appetite and

progressive weight loss are common in kidney disease.

Chronic renal failure is not reversible, but treatment aims to reduce the load on the remaining filter units (nephrons) and prevent further damage. Fluid intake should be encouraged. If the dog is vomiting, intravenous drips are necessary to provide the liquid needed to help the kidney work. Frequently taking the dog outside to help bladder emptying is helpful, too. The vet may advise a special diet, and will probably take repeated blood samples to monitor the kidneys' workload. A diet of high-biological-value protein, low in phosphate but rich in vitamin B, will be advised.

Diuretics to produce more urine may be used in some cases.

OTITIS EXTERNA

Ear diseases are more common in dogs such as the Springer, which have earflaps that hang down. When there is a lot of hair around the ear, the ventilation of the tube to the eardrum is poor and may encourage bacteria to multiply. When otitis occurs, a strong-smelling discharge develops and the dog shakes or tilts its head. Repeated scratching and head shaking may cause a swelling of blood underneath the skin of the earflap.

The presence of a grass seed in the ear canal should always be suspected in Springers that have been out in long grass in the summer months. After becoming trapped by the hair, the seed can quickly work its way down the ear canal and can even penetrate the eardrum. The spikes of the grass seed prevent it being shaken out of the ear and veterinary extraction of the seed is essential.

PARVOVIRUS

The form of the virus that infects younger dogs is most dangerous to the recently weaned puppy. Vaccination schedules are devised to protect susceptible dogs, and a vet's advice should be sought as to when, and how often, a parvo vaccine should be used in a particular locality. The virus has an incubation of about three to five days and attacks the bowels with a sudden onset of vomiting and diarrhoea. Blood may be passed, dehydration sets in, and

Kennel cough spreads quickly among dogs that live together.

sudden death is possible. Isolation from other puppies is essential. The replacement of fluids and electrolytes lost is urgent. Medication to stop vomiting, and antibiotics to fight against secondary bacteria, form part of the treatment. Once recovery is underway a smooth, bland diet may be provided.

PROSTATE DISEASE

Elderly Springer males that have not been castrated may show signs of straining, which may be thought to be a sign of constipation. However, an enlarged prostate gland at the neck of the bladder will often be the real cause. Most often it is a benign enlargement that causes pressure into the rectum, rather than blocking the bladder exit. Once diagnosed, hormone injections combined with a laxative diet may be very effective.

PYODERMA

A term used by some vets for a bacterial skin infection, pyoderma is a condition seen in Springer Spaniels often associated with wet, oozing skin known as 'wet eczema'. Treatment should be given to prevent licking and scratching, hair should be clipped away to encourage a dry surface where bacteria cannot multiply so readily, and an appropriate

MANGE

Several types of mange mites affect dogs and may be the cause of scratching, hair loss and ear disease. Sarcoptic mange causes the most irritation and is diagnosed by skin scrapings or a blood test. Demodectic mange is less of a problem and is diagnosed by skin scrapes or from plucked hairs. Otodectic mange occurs in the ears and the mite can be found in the wax. Cheyletiella is a surface mite of the coat. It causes white 'dandruff' signs and is diagnosed by coat brushing or sellotape impressions for inspection under a microscope. After identification, mite infections can be treated with medication provided by the vet. Repeat treatments after 10 to 14 days are needed to prevent reinfestation.

antibiotic can be used. If the bacteria tunnel inwards, it results in the furunculosis skin disorder, which is more difficult to treat.

PYOMETRA

This disease of the uterus can affect a bitch regardless of whether she has been bred from. The cause is a hormone imbalance that prepares the lining of the uterus for puppies. Fluid and mucus accumulate in the uterus, leading to acute illness if infected by bacteria. When a blood-stained, mucoid discharge comes out, often sticking to the hairs around the vulva, the disease is known as 'open pyometra'. It has been confused with a bitch coming on heat unexpectedly. It can be

more difficult to diagnose the cause of illness when there is no discharge present, known as 'closed pyometra'. Other ways of testing the patient for the uterus disorder may be employed by the vet in these cases. Although medical treatments are available, it is more usual to perform a hysterectomy, especially if the bitch has come to the end of her breeding career.

RABIES

The fatal viral infection is almost unknown in the UK, but it remains a cause of death in animals and some humans in parts of the world where a preventive vaccine is not in regular use. The disease attacks a dog's central nervous system. It is spread by infective saliva, usually following the bite of an animal developing the disease. Annual rabies vaccination is an important way of controlling the disease, and is essential for dogs travelling to and from the UK.

RINGWORM

This is a fungus affecting the skin and has nothing to do with worms. It acquired the name from the characteristic circular red marks it makes on the skin. It may appear as bald, scaly patches and will spread to children or adults handling the dog unless precautions are taken. Treatment will vary depending on the extent of the problem.

VESTIBULAR DISEASE

Older Springers may be subject to a head tilt, often with eye-flicking movements, known as nystagmus. At one time it was commonly diagnosed as a 'stroke' because of its sudden onset. The dog may circle or fall on one side, and then roll, unable to balance itself. Vestibular disease develops suddenly but, unlike the equivalent human stroke, there is no sign of bleeding in the brain. Recovery may take place slowly as the balance centre of the brain regains its use after one to three weeks. Treatment by the vet will assist a return to normal, although some dogs always carry their head with a tilt.

INHERITED DISORDERS

The English Springer Spaniel as a working breed is generally free of major problems, and many conditions have become much less prevalent due to good breeding and improved veterinary practices. However, the increased longevity of dogs makes it more likely that degenerative diseases will show themselves, though these can mostly be managed to allow a Springer to lead a normal life.

HIP DYSPLASIA

Hip dysplasia is a malformation of both the femoral head and

The English Springer's ears, which are long, feathered, and lie close to the head, should be inspected regularly.

acetabulum 'cup' of the hip, which results in lameness, pain and eventual arthritic changes. As an inherited disease of many working dogs, the breed average score for Springers in the UK (currently 13) is lower than many larger breeds, and on a par with most working gundogs. The basis of the control scheme is X-ray examination of young adult Springers in order to identify early signs of hip structure malformation. The X-rays are submitted for independent 'scores' under the BVA/Kennel Club scheme. In America, a similar scheme is run by the Orthopedic Foundation for Animals, although the scoring system is different. Anyone buying a puppy should enquire about the hip scores of the parents before completing the purchase. Your national kennel club will be able to give you more information about the schemes

and how to interpret the scores.

Control of the growing dog's weight, building up hindleg muscle, and avoiding injury as the skeleton develops, helps to control HD. The condition is exacerbated by excessive exercise, especially jumping up. Surgical treatments to correct hip abnormality may be carried out, but many cases can be controlled through regular exercise, muscle building, and the use of NSAIDs (non-steroidal, anti-inflammatory drugs).

ELBOW DYSPLASIA

Many dogs are affected by a condition known as OCD (osteochondritis dissecans). In Springers this disease may take one of two forms, the most common involving the inner side of the elbow joint with a small fracture of the coronoid process leading to a persisting foreleg lameness. The other form of OCD affects the shoulder joint and will also cause a permanent limp made worse by exercise.

EYE CONDITIONS

Abnormalities of the eyelids may be seen in the young, growing Springer. A condition known as entropion is where the edge of the eyelid rolls inwards and the lashes rub on the eyeball surface (the cornea), causing intense irritation and eye watering. Distichiasis and ectopic cilia are other eyelid problems of hereditary origins, but such diseases are amenable to surgery.

Conditions that affect the inside of the eye are more serious and can lead to blindness. Of particular importance is a group of inherited diseases known as progressive retinal atrophy (PRA), which are known to occur in certain families. Folding of the retina, known as retinal dysplasia (RD), is seen from time to time in Springers. Large areas of detachment of the retina will cause blindness.

Primary glaucoma is an inherited disorder in the Springer Spaniel (secondary glaucoma is the term used after some eye injury, or a dislocated lens). In glaucoma the eye becomes more prominent, as there is a rise of fluid pressure within the eyeball due to inadequate drainage of the fluid in the eye globe. This affects the retina, resulting in vision failure and possible permanent blindness. Pain is associated with glaucoma and urgent treatment is needed if the eye has sustained any injury.

Tests are available for a number of eye conditions, including PRA, RD and glaucoma, as part of a scheme run by the British Veterinary Association, the Kennel Club and the International Sheep Dog Society. The BVA/KC/ISDS Eye Scheme gives breeders the opportunity to test their breeding stock for these diseases, allowing them to use the resulting

The English Springer Spaniel is the ultimate companion dog – once you have owned a Springer you will never want to be without one.

information to eliminate or reduce the frequency of these diseases in their puppies. In America, a similar scheme is operated under the auspices of the Canine Eye Registration Foundation. More information can be obtained from the Kennel Club.

A good breeder who has their dogs tested regularly, will be able to show your certificates proving that the puppies' parents have been tested and are unaffected. Although it is not a guarantee that the puppy you buy will not develop eye problems later in life, it does make the possibility far less likely.

VON WILLEBRAND DISEASE

Blood-clotting diseases are known as haemophilia. In dogs these take several forms, such as Haemophilia A and Factor XI deficiency. Both these conditions, and reduced Factor VIII in the blood (known as von Willebrand)

resulting in a prolonged bleeding time, are all encountered in Springers but are fortunately quite rare. Blood tests will be required to measure the risk to the dog if an operation or dental extraction is planned.

COMPLEMENTARY THERAPIES

There are many complementary treatments available for dogs, such as physiotherapy, hydrotherapy, acupuncture and herbal treatments. In all cases you need to consult a person who has the experience and specialist knowledge of applying the treatments. Your Springer's vet should be informed, since some veterinary medicines should not be used when other remedies are involved. However, there are also vets who now provide a more holistic approach and offer complementary therapies alongside traditional treatment.

THE CONTRIBUTORS

THE EDITOR
CELIA WOODBRIDGE
(Crackerjanne) has owned English Springer Spaniels for 25 years. She developed an interest in breeding and exhibiting and is currently a breed club secretary and chairman of a breed rescue charity. These days, with her four children having flown the nest, she lives on Romney Marsh in Kent, with her long-suffering husband, six English Springers, three cats, a dozen chickens and a geriatric sheep – all of which live in total harmony!
See Chapter Three: An English Springer For Your Lifestyle and Chapter Seven: The Perfect English Springer Spaniel.

HARRY HARDWICKE (Hardhill)
While enjoying a distinguished career in the fire service, Harry Hardwicke has trained English Springer Spaniels for more than 30 years. He has trained, handled and made up ten Field Trial Champions along the way and represented England in the gundog working test at the CLA Game Fair, winning the event three times with different dogs. He served for 12 years on the Kennel Club Field Trial Committee, which he later chaired and was chairman of the Spaniel Club.
See Chapter One: Getting To Know The English Springer Spaniel.

MAUREEN READ (Brailea)
Maureen lives in Hampshire and is the archivist for the Southern English Springer Spaniel Club and serves on its committee. She is passionate about the breed and its history, and spends many hours in research and the care of the club's precious artefacts. She has owned, bred and exhibited English Springers for 29 years and has always greatly admired the black and white Cleavehill dogs of Jean Taylor, promising herself that one day she would own one. Maureen currently owns and shows a black and white Cleavehill bitch and her homebred son, Brailea Believe It. She is an ardent Liverpool F.C. supporter, and her dog is named Riise after one of the team. She also collects Maud Earl pictures, Springer artefacts and Lalique glass, when she can find the time!
See Chapter Two: The First English Springer Spaniels.

FRAN GLENDENNING (Plaiglen)
Fran shows and breeds under the Plaiglen affix and has made up a couple of show champions. Although the English Springer Spaniel is her first love, she has owned a Labrador Retriever, an Irish Setter and shown an English Pointer. Fran also breeds and show Cocker Spaniels. She has served on various committees from the 1980s onwards, including the Southern English Springer Spaniel Society, Hampshire Gundog, and latterly serves on the ESS Club of Scotland Committee. Fran has judged in Europe and in Australia, and she is soon to judge in the USA. Working with her partner, she now runs a very busy and successful boarding and quarantine kennels and cattery in Yorkshire.
See Chapter Four: The New Arrival

GARETH LAWLER (Roqfolly)
Gareth has been involved in ESS since 1983, and breeds and shows under the Roqfolly affix, making up three ESS in the UK and breeding several overseas champions. He is a committee member of the English Springer Spaniel Club of Wales. Gareth is a championship show judge of English and Welsh Springers and Cocker Spaniels. A former lecturer in Animal Science - including nutrition, he now devotes his time to running a busy boarding kennels in South Wales, with his wife Ceri.
See Chapter Five: The Best Of Care.

JULIA BARNES
Julia has owned and trained a number of different dog breeds, and is a puppy socialiser for Dogs for the Disabled. A former journalist, she has written many books, including several on dog training and behaviour. Julia is indebted to Jan Driver for her specialist knowledge on English Springer Spaniel training and behaviour.
See Chapter Six: Training and Socialisation.

DICK LANE BScFRAgSFRCVS
Dick qualified from the Royal Veterinary College in 1953 and then spent most of his time in veterinary practice in Warwickshire. He had a particular interest in Assistance Dogs: working for the Guide Dogs for the Blind Association and more recently for Dogs for the Disabled as a founder Trustee. Dick has been awarded a Fellowship of the Royal College of Veterinary Surgeons and a Fellowship of the Royal Agricultural Societies. He has recently completed an Honours BSc in Applied Animal Behaviour and Training, awarded by the University of Hull.
See Chapter Eight: Happy and Healthy.

USEFUL ADDRESSES

KENNEL & BREED CLUBS

UK

The Kennel Club
1 Clarges Street, London, W1J 8AB
Tel: 0870 606 6750
Fax: 0207 518 1058
Web: www.the-kennel-club.org.uk

To obtain up-to-date contact information for the following breed clubs, contact the Kennel Club:
• Anrim & Down Springer Spaniel Club
• English Springer Spaniel Club
• English Springer Spaniel Club of Northern Ireland
• English Springer Spaniel Club of Scotland
• English Springer Spaniel Club of Wales
• Lancashire & Cheshire English Springer Spaniel Club
• Midland English Springer Spaniel Society
• Northern English Springer Spaniel Society
• South Western English Springer Spaniel Society
• Southern English Springer Spaniel Society

USA

American Kennel Club (AKC)
5580 Centerview Drive,
Raleigh, NC 27606, USA.
Tel: 919 233 9767
Fax: 919 233 3627
Email: info@akc.org
Web: www.akc.org

United Kennel Club (UKC)
100 E Kilgore Rd, Kalamazoo,
MI 49002-5584, USA.
Tel: 269 343 9020
Fax: 269 343 7037
Web: www.ukcdogs.com/

English Springer Spaniel Field Trial Association, Inc.
Web: http://www.essfta.org/

For contact details of regional clubs, please contact the English Springer Spaniel Field Trial Association of America.

AUSTRALIA

Australian National Kennel Council (ANKC)
The Australian National Kennel Council is the administrative body for pure breed canine affairs in Australia. It does not, however, deal directly with dog exhibitors, breeders or judges. For information pertaining to breeders, clubs or shows, please contact the relevant State or Territory Controlling Body.

Dogs Australian Capital Territory
PO Box 815, Dickson ACT 2602
Tel: (02) 6241 4404
Fax: (02) 6241 1129
Email: administrator@dogsact.org.au
Web: www.dogsact.org.au

Dogs New South Wales
PO Box 632, St Marys, NSW 1790
Tel: (02) 9834 3022 or 1300 728 022 (NSW Only)
Fax: (02) 9834 3872
Email: info@dogsnsw.org.au
Web: www.dogsnsw.org.au

Dogs Northern Territory
PO Box 37521, Winnellie NT 0821
Tel: (08) 8984 3570
Fax: (08) 8984 3409
Email: admin@dogsnt.com.au
Web: www.dogsnt.com.au

Dogs Queensland
PO Box 495, Fortitude Valley Qld 4006
Tel: (07) 3252 2661
Fax: (07) 3252 3864
Email: info@dogsqueensland.org.au
Web: www.dogsqueensland.org.au

Dogs South Australia
PO Box 844
Prospect East SA 5082
Tel: (08) 8349 4797
Fax: (08) 8262 5751
Email: info@dogssa.com.au
Web: www.dogssa.com.au

Tasmanian Canine Association Inc
The Rothman Building
PO Box 116
Glenorchy Tas 7010
Tel: (03) 6272 9443
Fax: (03) 6273 0844
Email: tca@iprimus.com.au
Web: www.tasdogs.com

Dogs Victoria
Locked Bag K9
Cranbourne VIC 3977
Tel: (03)9788 2500
Fax: (03) 9788 2599
Email: office@dogsvictoria.org.au
Web: www.dogsvictoria.org.au

Dogs Western Australia
PO Box 1404
Canning Vale WA 6970
Tel: (08) 9455 1188
Fax: (08) 9455 1190
Email: k9@dogswest.com
Web: www.dogswest.com

INTERNATIONAL

Fédération Cynologique Internationale (FCI)/World Canine Organisation
Place Albert 1er, 13, B-6530 Thuin,
Belgium.
Tel: +32 71 59.12.38
Fax: +32 71 59.22.29
Web: www.fci.be/

TRAINING AND BEHAVIOUR

UK

Association of Pet Dog Trainers
PO Box 17, Kempsford, GL7 4WZ
Telephone: 01285 810811
Email: APDToffice@aol.com
Web: http://www.apdt.co.uk

Association of Pet Behaviour Counsellors
PO BOX 46, Worcester, WR8 9YS
Telephone: 01386 751151
Fax: 01386 750743
Email: info@apbc.org.uk
Web: http://www.apbc.org.uk/

USA

Association of Pet Dog Trainers
101 North Main Street, Suite 610
Greenville, SC 29601, USA.
Tel: 1 800 738 3647
Email: information@apdt.com
Web: www.apdt.com/

American College of Veterinary Behaviorists
College of Veterinary Medicine, 4474 Tamu, Texas A&M University
College Station, Texas 77843-4474
Web: http://dacvb.org/

American Veterinary Society of Animal Behavior
Web: www.avsabonline.org/

AUSTRALIA

APPT Australia Inc
PO Box 3122, Bankstown Square, NSW 2200,
Email: secretary@apdt.com.au
Web: www.apdt.com.au

Canine Behaviour
For details of regional behaviourists, contact the relevant State or Territory Controlling Body.

ACTIVITIES

UK

Agility Club
http://www.agilityclub.co.uk/

British Flyball Association
PO Box 990, Doncaster, DN1 9FY
Telephone: 01628 829623
Email: secretary@flyball.org.uk
Web: http://www.flyball.org.uk/

USA

North American Dog Agility Council
P.O. Box 1206, Colbert,
OK 74733, USA.
Web: www.nadac.com/

North American Flyball Association, Inc.
1333 West Devon Avenue, #512
Chicago, IL 60660

Tel/Fax: 800 318 6312
Email: flyball@flyball.org
Web: www.flyball.org/

AUSTRALIA
Agility Dog Association of Australia
ADAA Secretary, PO Box 2212,
Gailes, QLD 4300, Australia.
Tel: 0423 138 914
Email: admin@adaa.com.au
Web: www.adaa.com.au/

NADAC Australia (North American Dog Agility Council - Australian Division)
12 Wellman Street, Box Hill South, Victoria 3128, Australia.
Email: shirlene@nadacaustralia.com
Web: www.nadacaustralia.com/

Australian Flyball Association
PO Box 4179, Pitt Town, NSW 2756
Tel: 0407 337 939
Email: info@flyball.org.au
Web: www.flyball.org.au/

INTERNATIONAL

World Canine Freestyle Organisation
P.O. Box 350122, Brooklyn, NY 11235-2525, USA
Tel: (718) 332-8336
Fax: (718) 646-2686
Email: wcfodogs@aol.com
Web: www.worldcaninefreestyle.org

HEALTH

UK
Alternative Veterinary Medicine Centre
Chinham House, Stanford in the Vale,
Oxfordshire, SN7 8NQ
Tel: 01367 710324
Fax: 01367 718243
Web: www.alternativevet.org/

British Small Animal Veterinary Association
Woodrow House, 1 Telford Way,
Waterwells Business Park, Quedgeley,
Gloucestershire, GL2 2AB
Tel: 01452 726700
Fax: 01452 726701
Email: customerservices@bsava.com
Web: http://www.bsava.com/

Royal College of Veterinary Surgeons
Belgravia House, 62-64 Horseferry Road, London, SW1P 2AF
Tel: 0207 222 2001
Fax: 0207 222 2004
Email: admin@rcvs.org.uk
Web: www.rcvs.org.uk

USA
American Holistic Veterinary Medical Association
2218 Old Emmorton Road, Bel Air, MD 21015

Tel: 410 569 0795
Fax 410 569 2346
Email: office@ahvma.org
Web: www.ahvma.org/

American Veterinary Medical Association
1931 North Meacham Road, Suite 100,
Schaumburg, IL 60173-4360, USA.
Tel: 800 248 2862
Fax: 847 925 1329
Web: www.avma.org

American College of Veterinary Surgeons
19785 Crystal Rock Dr, Suite 305
Germantown, MD 20874, USA.
Tel: 301 916 0200
Toll Free: 877 217 2287
Fax: 301 916 2287
Email: acvs@acvs.org
Web: www.acvs.org/

AUSTRALIA
Australian Holistic Vets
Web: www.ahv.com.au/

Australian Small Animal Veterinary Association
40/6 Herbert Street, St Leonards, NSW 2065, Australia.
Tel: 02 9431 5090
Fax: 02 9437 9068
Email: asava@ava.com.au
Web: www.asava.com.au

Australian Veterinary Association
Unit 40, 6 Herbert Street, St Leonards, NSW 2065, Australia.
Tel: 02 9431 5000
Fax: 02 9437 9068
Web: www.ava.com.au

Australian College Veterinary Scientists
Building 3, Garden City Office Park,
2404 Logan Road, Eight Mile Plains, Queensland 4113, Australia.
Tel: 07 3423 2016
Fax: 07 3423 2977
Email: admin@acvs.org.au
Web: http://acvsc.org.au

ASSISTANCE DOGS

UK
Canine Partners
Mill Lane, Heyshott, Midhurst, GU29 0ED
Tel: 08456 580480
Fax: 08456 580481
Web: www.caninepartners.co.uk

Dogs for the Disabled
The Frances Hay Centre, Blacklocks Hill,
Banbury, Oxon, OX17 2BS
Tel: 01295 252600
Web: www.dogsforthedisabled.org

Guide Dogs for the Blind Association
Burghfield Common, Reading, RG7 3YG
Tel: 01189 835555
Fax: 01189 835433
Web: www.guidedogs.org.uk/

Hearing Dogs for Deaf People
The Grange, Wycombe Road, Saunderton, Princes Risborough, Bucks, HP27 9NS
Tel: 01844 348100
Fax: 01844 348101
Web: www.hearingdogs.org.uk

Pets as Therapy
14a High Street, Wendover, Aylesbury, Bucks. HP22 6EA.
Tel: 01845 345445
Fax: 01845 550236
Web: http://www.petsastherapy.org/

Support Dogs
21 Jessops Riverside, Brightside Lane, Sheffield, S9 2RX
Tel: 01142 617800
Fax: 01142 617555
Email: supportdogs@btconnect.com
Web: www.support-dogs.org.uk

USA
Therapy Dogs International
88 Bartley Road, Flanders, NJ 07836,.
Tel: 973 252 9800
Fax: 973 252 7171
Web: www.tdi-dog.o

Therapy Dogs Inc.
P.O. Box 20227, Cheyenne, WY 82003.
Tel: 307 432 0272.
Fax: 307-638-2079
Web: www.therapydogs.com

Delta Society - Pet Partners
875 124th Ave NE, Suite 101, Bellevue, WA 98005 USA.
Email: info@DeltaSociety.org
Web: www.deltasociety.org

Comfort Caring Canines
8135 Lare Street, Philadelphia, PA 19128.
Email: ccc@comfortcaringcanines.org
Web: www.comfortcaringcanines.org/

AUSTRALIA
AWARE Dogs Australia, Inc
PO Box 883, Kuranda, Queensland, 488..
Tel: 07 4093 8152
Web: www.awaredogs.org.au/

Delta Society — Therapy Dogs
Web: www.deltasociety.com.au